Calligraphy Today

HEATHER CHILD

Calligraphy Today

A survey of tradition and trends

WATSON-GUPTILL PUBLICATIONS, INC.
NEW YORK

Acknowledgements

My grateful acknowledgements are due to all who
have lent work for the illustrations and to the
Trustees of the British Museum, Victoria and
Albert Museum and Bodleian Library for per-
mission to reproduce from their collections of
manuscripts. I am grateful for advice given to me
by Mr Alfred Fairbank, C.B.E., and to fellow
members of the Society of Scribes and Illuminators
for their help, and to Miss Dorothy Abbe,
Mr P. W. Filby, Mr James Hayes and Mr Paul
Standard, in the U.S.A., for their generous
assistance.

© HEATHER CHILD MCMLXIII

Library of Congress Catalog Card Number: 64–14767
Published MCMLXIII by Studio Vista Books, London
Published MCMLXIV by Watson-Guptill Publications, Inc., New York, New York
Printed in Great Britain by Jarrold & Sons Ltd, Norwich

Contents

Selected List of Books
For the specialist and for the beginner

HISTORY

INTRODUCTION TO GREEK AND LATIN PALAEOGRAPHY
Sir Edward Maunde Thompson. Oxford University Press 1912

THE LEGACY OF THE MIDDLE AGES
Chapter on 'Handwriting' by E. A. Lowe. Oxford University Press 1926

ANCIENT WRITING AND ITS INFLUENCE   Professor B. L. Ullman. George Harrap & Co 1932

AN ILLUSTRATED HISTORY OF WRITING AND LETTERING   Jan Tschichold. Zwemmer 1946

MEISTERBUCH DER SCHRIFT   Jan Tschichold. Ravensburg 1952

THE ENCYCLOPAEDIA BRITANNICA   'Calligraphy' by Stanley Morison. 14th Edition

A BOOK OF SCRIPTS   Alfred Fairbank. King Penguin Books 1949

RENAISSANCE HANDWRITING   Alfred Fairbank and Berthold Wolpe. Faber and Faber 1960

TECHNIQUE

WRITING AND ILLUMINATING, AND LETTERING   Edward Johnston. John Hogg 1906

LETTERING   Graily Hewitt. Seeley Service & Co 1930

THE CALLIGRAPHER'S HANDBOOK   Edited by C. M. Lamb. Faber and Faber 1956

A HANDWRITING MANUAL   Alfred Fairbank. Faber and Faber (Revised Edition 1961)

THE ELEMENTS OF LETTERING   J. H. Benson and A. C. Carey. McGraw-Hill Book Co. Inc 1940

THE FIRST WRITING BOOK   Arrighi's *La Operina*. John Howard Benson. Oxford University Press 1955

LETTERING OF TODAY   Studio Publications 1937

MODERN LETTERING AND CALLIGRAPHY   Studio Publications 1954

PEN LETTERING   Ann Camp. Dryad Press 1958

CALLIGRAPHERS

EDWARD JOHNSTON   Priscilla Johnston. Faber and Faber 1959

EDWARD JOHNSTON AND ENGLISH LETTERING   Verlag für Schrift Kunde 1938

RUDOLF VON LARISCH AND HIS SCHOOL Verlag für Schrift Kunde. Heintze & Blanckertz. Berlin 1934

ANNA SIMONS   R. Oldenbourg Verlag München-Berlin. Verlag der Corona Zürich 1934

THE WORK OF JAN VAN KRIMPEN   John Dreyfus. The Sylvan Press 1952

JOHN HOWARD BENSON AND HIS WORK   Philip Hofer. The Typophiles. N.Y. 1957

Foreword

Calligraphy is the art of the pen. This book aims to be an illustrated survey of the tradition and trends in calligraphy since its revival at the beginning of the century. The illustrations, showing aspects of calligraphy today on both sides of the Atlantic, are its main feature. The active help of many scribes in Britain and overseas has been invaluable in furthering this aim. The illustrations include, firstly, works of formal calligraphy which are unique, such as manuscript books, scrolls, and framed pieces; secondly, calligraphy designed for reproduction; thirdly, exemplars, as aids to teaching. Informal handwriting is not included, as this subject has a literature of its own, but handwriting today is showing new life by the popularity of the italic hand and some of the illustrations show examples of italic both freely and gaily written.

In the choice of illustrations preference has been given where possible to work that has not been reproduced before. The selection has been limited by the fact that much fine penmanship does not show to its advantage in photographic reproduction and that works such as genealogical tables and decorative maps, do not reduce well. Any opportunity to see original manuscripts should not be missed, as the sharpness and texture of calligraphy and the richness of gilding on vellum requires to be seen to be appreciated. Students of calligraphy have a splendid inheritance in museums and there are excellent reproductions of historical manuscripts, but it is not so easy to see examples of good contemporary work. It is hoped that this book will help to stimulate interest in the wide range of formal writing being done today.

Calligraphy has been defined as 'beautiful writing'. The term covers formal writing with the edged-pen for formal occasions, but it also embraces informal writing, if this has beauty and legibility. The relevance of formal calligraphy to the needs of our generation may be questioned. It could be held that as we live in a mechanised age our thinking should be directed to making machines do the work and not our hands. This point of view ignores both the roots of our written culture and the need for creative expression. The alphabet we use—compounded as it is of history, principles, and expediency—was invented to transmit knowledge and record facts. It is a marvellous instrument and the civilisation we inherit is based on written records in all the many spheres of learning. After speech, the alphabet becomes the most vital bridge between man and man, and in literate societies all are taught to write. In earlier times, when books were entirely made by hand, they were rare and precious and it was normal for the skill of craftsmanship to be expended on the form of the letters and the arrangement and decoration of the page. Our Western alphabet goes back to classical Roman sources. The reed and quill were the ancestors of the metal edged pens used by calligraphers today.

The advent of printing changed the status of books and it may be asked why calligraphers exist today. The fact that they do is evidence of the vitality of this ancient craft. Calligraphy has a beauty and meaning that gives pleasure to many who do not practise the craft and, as the appreciation of fine writing increases, so will the realisation of its scope in everyday life. Calligraphy is used for unique works, such as rolls of honour, manuscript books and presentation addresses, and wherever typography, which is for mass production, is inappropriate.

The study and practice of calligraphy is a sound discipline for all who are concerned with letters: written, painted, incised or printed. The proportions of letters, the incidence of thicks and thins, their spacing and the arrangement of writing on the page provide a fundamental training for hand and eye. Contemporary hands should be free from archaism, but exhibit an understanding of historical styles. Technical expertise alone will not produce a notable piece of writing; unless a scribe is communicating a sense of quality, imagination and a lively grasp of the content of what he is transcribing, calligraphy tends to become a vehicle for exotic hands or mere ornamentation. As in all art where there is exceptional emphasis on decoration, it may carry the seeds of its own decline.

There is no doubt that calligraphers with vision and enterprise would, by experiment and practice, extend the range of this fascinating craft and it would enhance the prestige of calligraphy if the work of scribes was more widely known and used. It is heartening that calligraphy is now practised in many countries and it is to be hoped that increasing interchange of ideas and discussions will take place between scribes in Great Britain and scribes overseas.

Rector Magnifice

W. A. DWIGGINS
Chapter heading for an Alfred Knopf publication

Historical Note

The revival of calligraphy in this country cannot be properly appreciated without an understanding of the styles of writing in previous centuries on which the revival was based. The discovery of the beauty and discipline of these ancient hands engendered a creative vitality in calligraphers both in Britain and Germany and subsequently in America. Some examples from early writings are included therefore in this book, as it is upon these historical hands that many modern styles of calligraphy and type faces have been based directly or remotely.

The transitional letter forms in use today grew by a long process of development and modification. The Roman characters of classic times show clearly the formative influence of the tool used in making the letters; these tools were the flat brush and chisel on stone, the stylus on wax and clay, and the reed and quill on papyrus or skin. The arrangement of thick and thin strokes and the shape of the curves is largely determined by the instrument used to make the letters and, when writing, the angle at which it is held.

All styles of writing have had their time and their scribes, each reflecting something of the architecture and character of their age, and the people and places in which they developed. The Gothic letter, romantic, angular and ornamental, produces an entirely different feeling from the rounded, classic, well-balanced Roman letter, and the graceful cursive hands are in sharp contrast to both.

The perceptive calligrapher, enriched with a knowledge and understanding of the construction of the letter forms which are characteristic of these styles, will not merely copy them, but will select a style suited to his purpose and adapt it to the occasion, ceremonial, solemn or festive. He will produce a result which is contemporary in feeling and not archaic, but which is also based on an understanding of tradition.

The principal formal hands used in early book production were written in capital letters, or Majuscules; these in general consist of letters without ascending or descending strokes, written between two imaginary parallel lines.

In the 4th and 5th centuries A.D. books were written in Square Capitals, a hand clearly derived from the classical Roman inscriptional letters, which themselves have never been

9

surpassed in their grace, proportions and clarity, and of which the well-known Trajan column inscription is an outstanding example.

The Rustic Capitals of the same period were written more freely, the pen was held with a steeper angle of hairline, thus compressing the letters more closely together and making the down strokes thinner.

A third book-hand used by the Romans, also formed of capitals, was the Uncial. This more rounded hand was used from the 4th to the 8th century and was 'truly a penman's letter'.

During the same period, when the formal hands were used for writing books, the Roman cursive, or informal writing was developed from the capital letters and was used for documents, letters and similar commonplace purposes. Scribes writing rapidly would naturally alter the formal shapes of letters by force of economy and speed. These forms eventually became known as Minuscules or small letters, as distinct from Majuscules or capitals. Subsequently when printing was invented they were called lower-case letters, which tradition continues today.

To an intrusion of the Roman cursive everyday hand into the Uncial script letter we owe the development of the Half Uncial during the 7th century, marking an important step in the history of writing. From now onwards the small letters, with the introduction of ascending and descending strokes, are made between four imaginary lines in place of two. The pen was held with its edge straight to the line of writing.

All countries under the rule of Rome adopted these hands. The formal book-hands did not alter greatly in course of time but the cursive writing developed marked national characteristics of its own in Italy, Spain, France and England.

The spread of Christianity to Ireland from the 5th century brought the culture of Europe to that remote country and the Irish Half Uncial emerged, where it is seen at its best in the magical *Book of Kells*, written in the 8th century. From Ireland culture spread to Iona and Northumbria. The English Half Uncial which was a round hand developed there, and the magnificent *Lindisfarne Gospels*, completed in A.D. 698, and later found in the coffin of St Cuthbert, is the outstanding achievement in this hand.

The English Half Uncial was the first style of writing to be modernised by Edward Johnston and used as a copy-book hand for his students. He says of it that 'its essential roundness and formality discipline the hand. Its elegance has an aesthetic value and fits it for certain manuscript work, but unfits it for practical uses where thin parts are likely to damage (e.g. as a model for type or letters formed in any material, or to be read at a distance). It is in effect the 'straight-pen' form of the 'roman' small letter (that is, practically, the Roman Half Uncial). It therefore represents the ancestral type of small letter, and is a good basis for later hands.'

In the history of handwriting the Age of Charlemagne is of far-reaching importance.

In A.D. 789 Charlemagne, who did much to influence the religious and cultural life of his time, decreed the revision of Church books, with consequent activity in the monastic writing schools in France. Alcuin of York was appointed Abbot of the Monastery of Tours, where he remained for eight years until his death in 804, and where he encouraged the establishment of the clear, fluent script which came to be known as the Carolingian Minuscule. In its earliest form it had features that are cursive, such as a slight slope forward, and some of the letters made without pen lifts between the strokes. It was a hand of outstanding rhythmical beauty and importance; our lower-case printed letters today derive from it, and for centuries it remained the dominating hand of the West.

During the 10th century a particularly fine variation of the Carolingian Minuscule was used in southern England; it was strong and of developed formality. Edward Johnston considered this script 'an almost perfect model for a formal hand'. He wrote a modernised version using a slanted-pen which he called the Foundational Hand.

In France and England by the 12th century Carolingian was on the way to becoming Gothic. The 13th-century Gothic hand had compressed, pointed, and broken letters and though rich in pattern when at its best, it was tiring to the eyes. The Gothic styles in Germany have persisted until this century but are in retreat. It was fortunate for England that the dominant type faces have followed the Italian and not the medieval styles.

In Italy neither architecture nor letter-forms pursued the Gothic impulse to the full; both retained their rounded forms. The humanist scholars of the Renaissance searched for the classical authors and came upon manuscripts written in the Carolingian hands of the 11th and 12th centuries; this style they termed 'littera antiqua' and adopted it for their own use. The Renaissance versions of Carolingian hands are called Humanistic. In addition to their interest in manuscripts the humanists also observed and copied the classical Roman inscription letters and adopted them for writing, lettering and type.

Printing with moveable type had been invented in Germany about the middle of the 15th century, it is said by Gutenberg. The early German types were based on the formal Gothic book-hands. In Italy, however, type faces were inspired by the open and more legible styles of the revived Carolingian Minuscule and the Roman capital letters. It is hard to imagine more noble models for the design of type faces at the outset of printing and it is natural that the early printed books were modelled on manuscripts.

During the Renaissance in Italy a variant of the Carolingian hand was developed which we know as 'Italic'. Its characteristics were those of a cursive hand, the result of speed in writing, rhythm, and economy of effort. The hand, used both in manuscript books and in correspondence and for the numerous Papal briefs sent all over Christendom, was called at the end of the 15th century 'cancellaresca'; it also became the model for italic type faces.

The first Writing Book, *La Operina*, was produced in Rome in 1522 by Ludovico degli Arrighi of Vicenza. It offers instruction in using the cancellaresca hand and is printed from

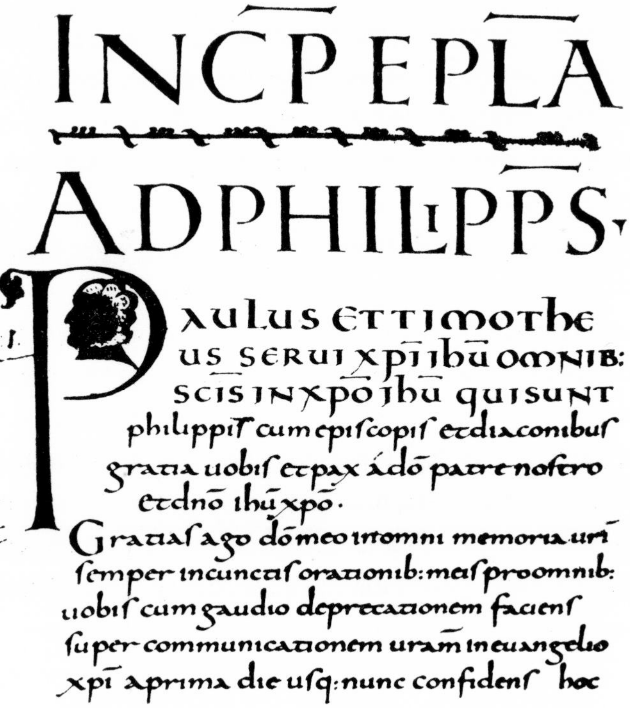

INCP EPLA

ADPHILPPS·

I·
Cap I.

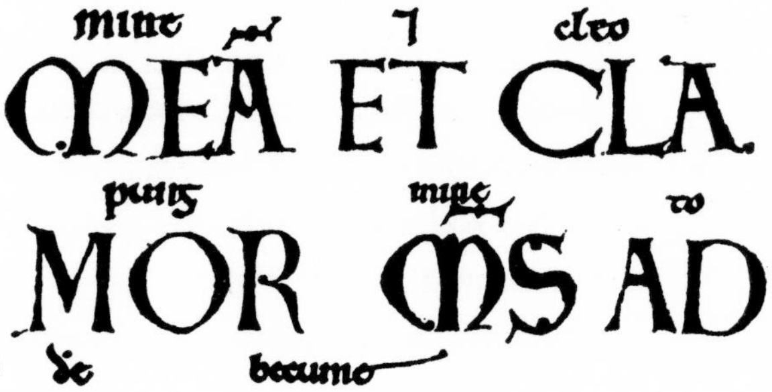

PAULUS ET TIMOTHE
US SERUI XPI IHU OMNIB:
SCIS IN XPO IHU QUISUNT
philippif cum episcopif etdiaconibuf
gratia uobif etpax ado patre noftro
etdno ihu xpo.

II

Gratiaf ago do meo ritomni memoria uri
femper incuncaf orationib: meaf proomnib:
uobif cum gaudio deprecationem facienf
fuper communicationem uram ineuangelio
xpi aprima die ufq: nunc confidenf hoc

8

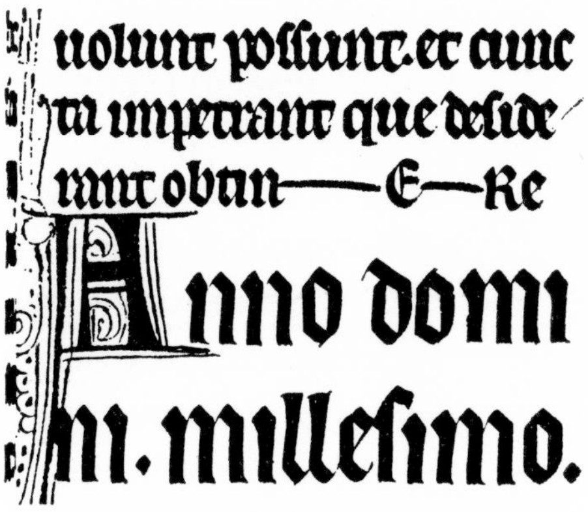

Confitebor dno nimif inore meo
& inmedio multorum
laudabo eum · ·:   ·:
qui aftitit adextrif pauperif
ut faluam faceret

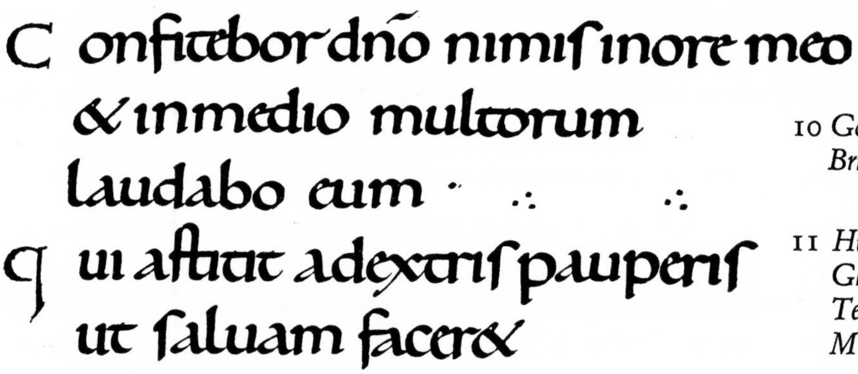

9

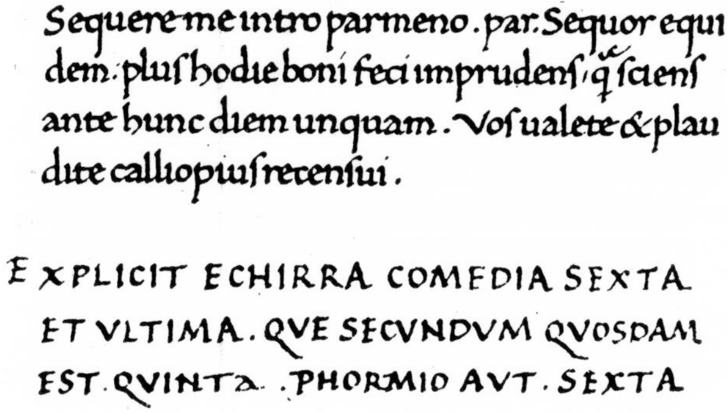

Sequere me intro parmeno. par. Sequor equi
dem. pluf hodie boni feci imprudenf q̃ fcienf
ante hunc diem unquam. Vof ualete & plau
dite calliopiuf recenfui.

EXPLICIT ECHIRRA COMEDIA SEXTA.
ET VLTIMA. QVE SECVNDVM QVOSDAM
EST. QVINTA. PHORMIO AVT. SEXTA

II

---

noluntr poffuntr. et cunc
ta impetrantr que defide
runt obtin — E — Re

Anno domi
ni. millefimo.

10

8 *Roman capitals, Uncials and*
Carolingian minuscules from the
Alcuin Bible, Tours,
9th century.
British Museum Add. MS. 10546

9 *English 10th-century hand. From*
a Psalter written in southern
England about A.D. 975.
British Museum Harl. MS. 2904

10 *Gothic 13th-century writing.*
British Museum Egerton 2569

11 *Humanistic script written by*
Gherardo del Ciriagio, 1466.
Terence, Comedies. Bodleian
MS. E.D. Clarke 28

12 *Carolingian Versals. British*
Museum Arundel 60

MEA ET CLA.

MOR MS AD

12

13

engraved wood-blocks. It has been an inspiration to modern calligraphers, as may be seen from illustrations in this book. Arrighi followed *La Operina* a year later with a second book of model hands *Il Modo*. In 1524 and 1544 Tagliente and Palatino published their Writing Books. The popularity of these aids to good writing encouraged similar exemplars to be produced in other countries.

With the widespread and increasing use of printing, books ceased to be written by hand. The quality of handwriting in everyday use also declined. The earlier aim of the printer had been to produce books resembling those written in formal hands. Handwriting became debased when, with the aid of the flexible pointed nib, it attempted to imitate the style of engraved letters.

By the end of the 19th century the creative arts and crafts were at a low ebb. Both type design and book production had seriously deteriorated. It was at this time that the vitalising influence of both John Ruskin and William Morris began to be felt. Morris's campaign for the ideals and recognition of craftsmanship came to fruition in the founding of the Arts and Crafts Movement.

The Revival of Calligraphy in Great Britain

William Morris was born in 1834 and died in 1896. He was a poet, romance writer and Socialist, and also a master of many crafts; indeed he was the father of the Arts and Crafts Movement, which was born of the political and artistic aspirations of that period. It was a revolt on a practical level against the ugly shoddiness of the products of the Industrial Revolution.

Morris made designs for wall-papers, glass, textiles, tapestries and print. His sense of craftsmanship soon led him to study the writings of old manuscripts, and he owned personally several fine early manuscripts. Between the years 1870 and 1876 he experimented with writing and decorating books in the style of the medieval and Renaissance scribes, a Horace, now in the Bodleian, a Virgil and two copies of Omar Khayyám among them. Some of these manuscript books were exhibited in the first exhibition of the Arts and Crafts Exhibition Society in 1888.

Two years later Morris founded the Kelmscott Press at Hammersmith with Emery Walker, who was an antiquary, a process engraver and typographical expert. In many ways the Kelmscott Press was the crowning achievement of Morris's life, and for which he designed type founts, ornamental letters and borders. Fifty-three books were produced by the Kelmscott Press of which the most famous is the *Chaucer*. Between them Morris and T. J. Cobden-Sanderson, who founded the Doves Press in 1890, raised the standard of book production from the low state into which it had fallen: following their success other private presses were started in England and on the Continent: many of the books produced were outstandingly beautiful, and calligraphers were commissioned to design for them both type and decorative or written initials.

Cobden-Sanderson was himself a binder and printer and a pioneer in the Arts and Crafts Movement of the eighties. In his treatise *The Book Beautiful* he emphasises the fact that Morris was a calligrapher and an illuminator before he became a printer. However, the influence Morris exerted was greater in the field of printed books than in manuscripts. His ideals of simplicity, beauty and fitness in the crafts were much in advance of his period.

Ruskin said of him, 'Morris is beaten gold—the most versatile man of his time.'

Victorian penmen in their formal writing used a form of Gothic script. With a fine-pointed, steel nib they painstakingly drew skeleton letters which they then filled in with a brush. It is not surprising that the writing in medieval manuscripts was thought to be the similar work of patient monks, set to copy slowly and laboriously sacred books for prelates and princes. The theory and technique of calligraphy was little known when Edward Johnston began to study the pen shapes of letters in the British Museum.

Edward Johnston, C.B.E., was born on 11th February 1872. In 1897 he turned from the study of medicine at Edinburgh, owing to delicate health, and from then onwards devoted himself to the study and practice of calligraphy until his death on 26th November 1944.

Johnston was fortunate in having the help of W. R. Lethaby, Sydney Cockerell and Robert Bridges at an early stage in his new career. Sydney Cockerell (later Sir Sydney Cockerell) had been William Morris's secretary and was himself an authority on ancient manuscripts; he pointed out to Johnston the finest specimens in the British Museum and told him of Morris's own researches. Johnston carried out his enquiries with the perception of a craftsman, scientist and philosopher. He rediscovered the principles on which formal writing had been developed, the tools and materials used and the correct preparation of them. He discovered that the nature and form of a letter was determined by the nature and form of the pen that made it, that an edged-pen makes thick and thin strokes according to direction and not pressure and that the size of the letter is in direct ratio to the breadth of the edged-pen making it. He found out how to cut and sharpen reeds and quills, the angle at which to trim the chisel edge of the pen and how to hold the pen in relation to the horizontal line, in order that it should make the desired shapes of the letters when writing. He experimented with preparing the surface of skins on which to write and also with inks and pigments.

It is hard to realise now when all these things are known to every student of calligraphy that they could have been forgotten. They were momentous discoveries.

In 1899 Johnston was asked by Professor Lethaby to take a class in 'Illuminating' at the newly formed L.C.C. Central School of Arts and Crafts, which was then in Upper Regent Street, London. Lethaby had been a young friend of William Morris and had played a part in initiating the Arts and Crafts Movement; he established what they had started and a whole generation of craftsmen owe their training in this fine tradition to him.

Johnston's class started with seven or eight students, including T. J. Cobden-Sanderson, who was considerably older than Johnston; Eric Gill, then a very young man who subsequently became renowned as a sculptor, engraver and letterer; Noel Rooke, who later engraved illustrations for *Writing & Illuminating, & Lettering*; Douglas Cockerell's wife and Emery Walker's daughter. Within a year their number had increased and included Louise Lessore, who married Alfred Powell; Graily Hewitt, Lawrence Christie, Percy Smith and Florence Kingsford, who became known for her illuminations and married Sydney Cockerell.

Priscilla Johnston in writing a life of her father, *Edward Johnston*, published in 1959, says of these early students they had 'every reason to regard themselves as pioneers. Together they were a band of explorers in an unknown country . . . Johnston's goal at this time—even more than to establish himself—was to establish the craft. He envisaged a sort of guild of calligraphers, all studying, experimenting and making discoveries which they would then all share.' A short-lived Society of Calligraphers was formed. Percy Smith was the Honorary Secretary and the Executive consisted of Eric Gill, Edward Johnston, Philip Mortimer and Allan Vigers.

In 1901 Johnston started his classes at the Royal College of Art at South Kensington. Lethaby had been appointed Professor of Design at the College, and it was an entirely new idea for writing and lettering to form an integral part of art education. Johnston's classes soon became enormous and he had to devise a means of mass instruction. He illustrated his lectures by remarkable blackboard demonstrations which were an inspiration to all who attended them. Fortunately this valuable teaching, committed to the fugitive medium of the blackboard, was recorded by one of his students, Violet Hawkes, who, with great foresight, made a photographic record of them.

To help his students Johnston used instruction sheets which he wrote himself in hecto-graph ink and by this means reproduced the limited number of copies required. Later the Pepler Sheets, partly written by hand and partly printed, were produced for the use of his students.

In the early years of the century only Edward Johnston and Graily Hewitt were capable of teaching calligraphy, and when Birmingham College of Art wanted to begin a class on the subject Ernest Treglown came to London especially to learn from Johnston. Before long Leicester College of Art had a lettering class, and in time the subject became an integral part of many art schools in London and in the provinces.

In 1906 Johnston's manual *Writing & Illuminating, & Lettering* was published. This classic textbook is indispensable to students of calligraphy and to all who are interested in the theory as well as the practice of the craft. Sir Sydney Cockerell said of it, 'Johnston's handbook is a masterpiece, immensely instructive and stimulating. And not only technically helpful, for the reader is conscious all the time of being brought in touch with a rare and fine spirit. *Writing & Illuminating, & Lettering* won him disciples and followers not only in this country, but in Germany, where he had a powerful advocate in one of his best pupils Anna Simons, in America and even as far as Australia.'

In 1909 a portfolio of *Manuscript & Inscription Letters* was published for schools and for the use of craftsmen. The sample alphabets were based upon Johnston's earlier class sheets and included plates by Eric Gill.

All his life Edward Johnston searched for truth in his work. He analysed and experimented with each important style of historic writing in turn, until he had become familiar with the shapes and relative proportions of the letters and had a complete understanding of how to manipulate the edged-pen in order to make these hands his own.

He taught his first pupils Uncials and Half Uncials and soon added—to the surprise of his students who thought they had learnt it all—his slanted-pen hand adapted from a 10th-century Winchester psalter. This was later to become his 'Foundational Hand' as he termed it, the basis of his teaching and the principal formal hand he used himself. These were followed by built-up Versals and Roman capitals, and later on Roman small letters and versions of italic which sprang from his experiments by compressing and slanting the Foundational Hand. Towards the end of his life he experimented with a sharpened italic which was Gothic in form.

Johnston's own work as a craftsman was much sought after. He was commissioned to make addresses, rolls of honour, service books, wedding presents and the like, by public bodies and private patrons; the Communion Service for a Hastings church, a Coronation Address to King Edward VII and the Fishmongers' Scrolls were among them. His output was small and his problem was always to get the work completed. Probably the most important and largest manuscript book he ever undertook was the Keighley Roll of Honour: this was written in 1924, but most of the manuscripts he made were in the form of small booklets. His commissioned works were usually magnificent broadsides, sometimes decorated with heraldry and burnished gold, such as the Freedom Scrolls he made for the Livery Companies of the City of London. His writing has an inner vitality which comes from his genius for combining and contrasting size, form and colour to make a unity of the whole. His pen strokes are sharp, direct and swift, the letters display an architectural quality and above all his integrity. He aimed at perfection and was always finding fault with his own work.

Between the years 1910 and 1930 Johnston designed initial letters and types for Count Harry Kessler of the Cranach Press in Germany. In 1916 he was commissioned by Frank

Pick to design a special type for the use of the London Transport Services. The result was a block letter alphabet based on classical Roman proportions—Johnston's sans-serif— forerunner of many sans-serif founts, including that of his pupil and friend Eric Gill, the Gill Sans type designed some years later for the Monotype Corporation.

Johnston revealed his unparalleled genius as a scribe in his own work, and as a teacher he exerted an immense influence for good upon letter forms in England and on the Continent, where his influence was probably greatest in Germany. It was not long after its publication that the impact of *Writing & Illuminating, & Lettering* was felt in America. The founding of the Society of Scribes and Illuminators in England in 1921 was the direct outcome of his teaching. Sir Francis Meynell said of Edward Johnston, 'He was one of the few really great men of our time.'

William Graily Hewitt, O.B.E., was born in 1864 and died in 1952. He studied law and was called to the bar in 1889, but finding no satisfaction in his profession he turned to writing and the study of early manuscripts comparatively late in life. On the advice of Sydney Cockerell he became one of Johnston's first pupils, and in 1901 he succeeded Johnston at the Central School of Arts and Crafts, where he taught for more than thirty years. In his teaching he developed Johnston's methods, but he was essentially a book scribe and his outlook was different; his particular interest lay with the Italian Renaissance styles of writing.

After the First World War he and his assistants prepared many memorials mostly in manuscript form for Public Schools, Inns of Court, Regiments, Public Companies and the House of Lords. He also wrote out the Letters Patent of Nobility and other important documents for the Crown Office and the Home Office.

Graily Hewitt's greatest achievement was his recovery of the craft of laying and burnishing gold leaf. The illuminated pages of medieval manuscripts owe much of their magnificence to the brilliance of pure gold leaf which may still retain its beauty and burnish even after hundreds of years. When the art of formal writing declined, following the invention of printing, the allied crafts of gilding in manuscripts deteriorated also and the relevant skills were practically forgotten. With the revival of calligraphy at the beginning of this century the opportunity for the use of burnished gold and illumination returned.

Graily Hewitt conducted a series of experiments over many years in order to rediscover the composition of the gesso used under the gold leaf as a raising preparation. He based these researches on the frequently obscure recipes and directions of Cennino Cennini. The unsurpassed gilding in Hewitt's own manuscripts, some wholly written in the gesso and gilded and burnished, testify to the success of these preparations and to his skill in using them. Some details of his methods are described in his own book *Lettering* and in his chapter on gilding in Johnston's *Writing & Illuminating, & Lettering*.

Graily Hewitt admired the humanistic manuscripts of the 15th century and particularly those of Antonio Sinibaldi and Johannes Andreas de Colonia. It was from humanistic scripts that some early printing types derived.

Hewitt developed a style of illumination which grew out of the initial letter, often of burnished gold, and he also took the so-called 'white vine' of the 15th-century Italian manuscripts as a model for ivory-coloured scroll work set against panels of jewelled colour. He aimed at a style of illumination that while allowing of some variation would yet be consistent throughout a manuscript, and be adaptable enough to fit any space. He used decoratively such English trees and shrubs as the oak with gilded acorns, the chestnut, beech, rose and ivy. These were for the solid decoration, and to them he added a filigree of simpler flower forms, such as speedwell, clover, pimpernel and bindweed, enlivened with butterflies and birds. This manner of illumination was exquisitely carried out by Madelyn Walker and Ida Henstock among others.

Graily Hewitt and his assistants came near to the medieval concept of a Scriptorium or team of craftsmen, each contributing his skill to the making and decorating of fine manuscripts.

The *Oxford Copy Books* were published in 1916; they were an early attempt to provide a model for handwriting. The writing is a fine italic script based on the 16th-century hands, but the letters have no joins and it is not truly a cursive hand. In 1932 Hewitt's *Treyford Writing Cards* were published and in 1938 his *Handwriting: Everyman's Craft*.

When he retired from teaching Graily Hewitt formed the Manuscript Club, where his past students and other people interested in the subject could meet together and discuss matters of common interest.

The Revival of Italic Handwriting

With the rapidly increasing appreciation of the importance of good lettering, following the teaching of Edward Johnston, it is understandable that there should arise at the same time a discontent with the low standard of ordinary handwriting. The virtues of the italic cursive hands and their suitability for use today began to be recognised.

Before the end of the last century William Morris had attempted to use an italic script in writing some of his manuscripts. The wife of Dr Robert Bridges, the Poet Laureate, published *A New Handwriting for Teachers* in 1898: one of the earliest protests against bad handwriting, it contained an Italianised Gothic hand, or italic as it would be called today. Edward Johnston included an italic hand among the illustrations in *Writing & Illuminating, & Lettering* in 1906. He thought it showed possibilities for improving current handwriting, a thing which he considered would be 'one of the most practical benefits of the study of calligraphy'.

After the First World War considerable research was made into the humanistic scripts by palaeographers, typographers and calligraphers; these included Professor B. L. Ullman, Stanley Morison, the late James Wardrop, A. F. Johnson and Alfred Fairbank. The variety of these interests led to a broader appreciation of italic and the revived use of italic handwriting began to gain ground, although until recent years the teaching of the system in schools was slight.

Alfred Fairbank, c.b.e., who was a pupil of Graily Hewitt and Lawrence Christie, was at first attracted by the formal book-hands, but as early as 1923 he began to take particular interest in italic. The result of his early researches and experiments with these hands led to the publication in 1932 of the *Woodside Writing Cards* and in 1935 to the *Barking Writing Cards*, which later became known as the *Dryad Writing Cards*. These exemplars illustrate a model cursive hand allowing the use of joins. Among the influences in making them were the writing manuals of G. A. Tagliente, who was a Venetian, and F. Lucas, a Spaniard. These Cards together with the edged dip-pens he had had made were a basis for teaching italic handwriting in schools.

In 1932 Alfred Fairbank's book *A Handwriting Manual* was published, the forerunner of many books on italic handwriting. It is the outstanding work on the subject both for the teacher and the adult who wishes to remodel his writing in the italic style. Its influence spread rapidly on both sides of the Atlantic. His later models are the *Beacon Writing Books*.

The range of Alfred Fairbank's interest and research is indicated by *A Book of Scripts* and *Renaissance Handwriting*, the latter made jointly with Berthold Wolpe. The notable part he has played in the cause of italic handwriting has possibly obscured the true appreciation of his skill as a formal calligrapher. The manuscripts he wrote and gilded between the years 1924 and 1939 for Mr St John Hornby and others are seldom seen. These elegant and dignified books were written on vellum in roman and italic hands in leisure hours from his work in the Civil Service. They are the fruit of a successful collaboration with Louise Powell who made the illuminations. Her visual imagination was so strong that she could paint directly on the page without preliminary drawing.

Shortly after the Second World War public interest in the reform of handwriting in general, and the adoption of a contemporary italic script in particular, was stimulated by articles and letters in the Press, lectures and exhibitions. In 1952 Alfred Fairbank, President of the Society of Scribes and Illuminators, urged that the time had come for the formation of a new society to canalise and foster this interest, and in that year the Society of Scribes and Illuminators instituted the Society for Italic Handwriting. This junior Society was to be a forum for discussion and lectures on the subject, and a means of assistance to adults seeking to remodel their own handwriting and to teachers in schools, always with the purpose of raising standards. The new society rapidly gained a large international membership and its scope increased.

The italic scripts of today fall into two catagories in England: those that derive from Edward Johnston and those that derive from the Italian Renaissance. Johnston's italics, requiring many pen-lifts like other formal book-hands, were developed ultimately from his Foundational Hand. A late version, which he called 'heavy italics', might be thought of as a gothicised italic. The cursive italic in its *set* form (springing from the scribes and writing-masters of the Renaissance) is used for various special purposes for its beauty and fitness and as copy-book exemplars; it is as precisely made as the Johnstonian italic except that pen-lifts are reduced. The *free* cursive italic, with use of many joins, is primarily a legible and rapid hand, which offers a graceful alternative to the more slipshod and unconsidered styles of handwriting. In the past few years many people have found the genuine pleasures of crafts-manship in adopting this hand for their own everyday use.

The Revival of Calligraphy on the Continent

Concurrently with the calligraphic movement which took place in England at the beginning of this century, similar but independent movements began on the Continent. The chief exponents of the far-reaching reforms in writing were Edward Johnston in England, Rudolf von Larisch in Vienna and, later, Rudolf Koch in Germany. The aims of these men were to raise the arts of writing and lettering from the debased state to which they had sunk and to give a significance once more to the work of the scribe. The extent to which these aims were achieved can be seen in penmanship and letter-forms everywhere today.

Rudolf von Larisch, who was sixteen years senior to Edward Johnston, was born in Verona in 1856 and died in Vienna in 1934. He was the gifted and musical son of an army officer and was early orphaned. For many years he was an official in the Chancery of the Austrian Emperor Franz Josef, archivist of the Order of the Toison d'Or and Keeper of the Hapsburg Records. Such appointments gave him ample opportunity for the study of historical manuscripts, in a country where long-established cultures from East and West had influenced styles of writing over the centuries. The debased penmanship of the more recent records so disgusted him that he became fired with a passionate desire for hand-writing reform. He published a pamphlet *Zierschriften im Dienst der Kunst* (Decorative Writing and Lettering in Art) and this led to his appointment as lecturer in Lettering at the Vienna School of Art in 1902 and was the beginning of his teaching career: it was just a year after Edward Johnston had begun teaching at the Royal College of Art in London.

Rudolf von Larisch wrote numerous articles in the Press in an effort to awaken the interest of the public and he produced portfolios with reproductions of examples of fine writing. His most important work *Unterricht in Ornamentaler Schrift* (A Manual of Instruction in Decorative Writing and Lettering) appeared in 1906 and had a notable influence in German-speaking countries.

Von Larisch felt the basis of calligraphy to be a natural desire for creative self-expression and that penmanship therefore was of genuine educational value. He did not consider calligraphy as an end in itself, a mere exercise in virtuosity. He encouraged his students to develop their inventiveness and to carry out experiments in writing and lettering on a variety of materials, such as wood, glass, metal, pottery and textiles, to discover the varying techniques and methods of expression each demanded. This was in contrast to Johnston's teaching which was based mainly on the study of traditional hands and on the principles arising from his researches. Von Larisch felt that the perceptive calligrapher should express feeling in his work, that the pattern of the written letters on the page and the rhythm of the writing itself should harmonise, and that the whole work should express a unity of emotion. He taught the proper handling and use of all kinds of writing tools, many of which he developed by experiment, in co-operation with Rudolf Blanckertz of the well-known firm of pen manufacturers, himself a tireless worker for calligraphy and founder of the Handwriting Museum in Berlin.

Although Rudolf von Larisch and Edward Johnston started independently to study, and their methods of teaching differed, their aims and the conclusions they arrived at were sympathetically related, and when they met in London in 1909 they found a mutual understanding and liking for one another.

Rudolf von Larisch had a number of assistants, the best known being Dr Otto Hurm and Hertha Ramsauer, who became Von Larisch's wife and who carried on his work in Switzerland after his death.

Anna Simons, who was born in 1871 and died in 1951, came of a legal family. As women art students were not permitted in Prussia in 1896 she went to London to train at the Royal College of Art, at the time when the influence of the Arts and Crafts Movement was growing, with London the centre of it. When Edward Johnston began teaching at the College in 1901 she joined his class and quickly became one of the best students he ever taught. He said of her: 'She had a natural aptitude for the work and a sincerity and directness of outlook which enabled her to master the essential elements very rapidly, and later to develop them into her own practical and beautiful work.'

After obtaining her diploma at the Royal College of Art Anna Simons returned to Germany where she began successfully to teach Johnston's methods. In 1905 the Prussian

Ministry of Commerce arranged a lettering course for art teachers at Düsseldorf, the first of its kind. Count Harry Kessler, already impressed by Johnston's work when they had met in London the year before, saw this as a further opportunity of introducing his teaching into Germany. Johnston himself was not available, but he recommended Anna Simons, who conducted the course with outstanding success. The Germans were already alive to the revival of fine writing, lettering and printing, and great interest was aroused by this lettering course. It became a yearly affair and Johnston's methods were spread throughout the country both by Anna Simons and her pupils.

There was a demand for a translation of Edward Johnston's manual *Writing & Illuminating, & Lettering*. This immensely difficult task was carried out by Anna Simons in 1910 with complete success, and two years later she translated into German the text of his portfolio of *Manuscript and Inscription Letters*.

In 1912 Edward Johnston was persuaded to go to Dresden where he gave an impressive lecture on the technical side of his work, the history and development of letters and his own philosophy, at the Fourth International Congress in Art Education. Anna Simons stood beside him translating his remarks, but the outstanding feature of his lecture was the black-board demonstration which caused a sensation. When visiting art schools on the Continent some years later Sir William Rothenstein was surprised to find 'that it was not Mr Kipling but Mr Johnston who was the best-known Englishman in most of the foreign countries he had visited'.

At this period the Germans were moving away from their traditional Gothic and beginning to use Roman types; Stanley Morison wrote in 1926: 'the school of calligraphers practising the teaching of Johnston and Gill, which has arisen since the year 1905, has in its hands the whole of German type design, with the exception of the cruder kinds of advertising letter'. This close link between calligraphy and typography has persisted on the Continent, where centres of printing are more widespread than in England and where there has been a closer liaison between art schools, type foundries, printing houses, and the workshops of craftsmen. It is to be regretted that the early relationship between calligraphy and typography appears to have worn very thin in England today.

Rudolf Koch of Offenbach, was born in 1874 and died in 1934. He was a calligrapher and a type designer, skilled in many crafts, and an inspiring teacher. He studied in Nuremburg, Hanau, Munich and Leipzig, then the most important printing centres in Germany. He worked for the Klingspor type foundry in Offenbach and taught lettering at the School of Arts and Crafts there. His students and their work were of profound importance to him and his teaching and type designing helped the development of his own talents. He re-established a close relationship between printing and penmanship and the most successful part of his creative work were his type designs. He believed that no serious calligrapher can afford to overlook the making of manuscript books, for only there will he find all the questions and only there can he prove his art in answering them. As a calligrapher Koch was at his best and most inventive with the decorative patterning of the Gothic forms of letters.

In 1918 the group of Offenbach Penmen was organised and later this was developed into the Workshop Community where Koch and his assistants produced together many important works: lettering, woodcuts, weaving, metal work, embroideries and block-books printed on Japanese paper. These were the products of the whole group of creative craftsmen working together with this remarkably versatile and genuine craftsman. All Koch's assistants have had one thing in common, whatever their other skills may be, and that is a fundamental training in lettering.

Koch's Master Students have made distinguished reputations as teachers and craftsmen, among them being Friedrich Heinrichsen, calligrapher; Fritz Kredel, wood-engraver and book illustrator, and Warren Chappell, book designer and illustrator, both these craftsmen are working in New York; and Berthold Wolpe, who was trained as a silversmith and is now a well-known designer in London.

STUART BARRIE
*Monogram from a
wedding invitation*

Present Practice of Calligraphy in Great Britain

A direct outcome of the teaching and practice of Edward Johnston was the formation of the Society of Scribes and Illuminators in 1921 through the initiative of Louisa Puller. In its early days the Society was a student body composed mainly of those associated with the Central School of Arts and Crafts, where Graily Hewitt and Lawrence Christie were teaching writing and illuminating. The Society was founded for 'the advancement of the Crafts of Writing and Illumination by the practice of these for themselves alone. That the aim of the Society should be zealously directed toward the production of books and documents wholly handmade: regarding other application as subordinate, but not excluding it.'

When the Society instituted Honorary Membership by invitation 'to those who have assisted in the advancement of the Crafts, or have been of service to the Society', it was obvious that Edward Johnston should be elected the first Honorary Member. He continued to be the inspiration and mentor of its members and the majority have followed his methods in their own work.

In the early years Research Groups were formed which carried out useful technical experiments. A unique and valuable Record Book has been kept, in which the findings of these experiments and the resulting discussions have been recorded. In 1956, the fiftieth anniversary of the publication of *Writing & Illuminating, & Lettering*, a book of essays on various aspects of calligraphy and illumination was published, *The Calligrapher's Handbook*, which was prepared by members of the Society of Scribes and Illuminators with wide experience in the crafts, and was edited by the Rev. C. M. Lamb, who for many years has been Treasurer to the Society.

Many distinguished lecturers have addressed the Society's Open Meetings, on palaeography, heraldry and other subjects related to calligraphy and illumination, and general meetings with technical discussions are held during the year for members.

Important exhibitions have been organised in England and abroad by the Society. In 1930 and 1938 exhibitions were held in the U.S.A., at the invitation of the American Institute of Graphic Arts, and were shown in New York, Boston and Chicago, as well as the Universities of Yale and Pittsburg. In 1931 work was sent to the Salon International du Livre d'Art at the Petit-Palais des Beaux Arts in Paris, and in 1932 calligraphy was shown in Copenhagen at the British Industrial Art Exhibition. In London exhibitions were organised by the Society in 1931 at the Victoria and Albert Museum, and five years later at the Architectural Association. A series of notable exhibitions of calligraphy and illumination have been held in 1951, 1956 and 1961 at the Crafts Centre of Great Britain.

Today the Society is a body of professional calligraphers, most of whom were either pupils of Edward Johnston himself or of his pupils. Among those who have carried on his teaching methods are Dorothy Mahoney, Irene Wellington, Margaret Alexander, Daisy Alcock, T. W. Swindlehurst, Rosemary Ratcliffe and the late M. C. Oliver.

Probably the most outstanding feature of the work of calligraphers in Britain today is the production of ceremonial works of public and private bodies for expressions of honour and appreciation. 'Formal occasions call for formal scripts' and relevant decoration, for which the pomp of heraldry and the richness of burnished gold are frequently appropriate. A high level of technical skill has been reached in these unique works and many of them are transcribed on vellum in the form of manuscript books, scrolls or broadsides. In this field Margaret Alexander, Ida Henstock and Dorothy Hutton transcribe and illuminate important documents for the Crown Office. While most calligraphers carry out their own decoration, there have been notable collaborations between scribe and gilder and scribe and illuminator, and several are illustrated in this book. The most striking example of recent collaboration has been the Rolls of Honour for the Royal Air Force and the American Air Force, at St Clement Danes Church. Thirteen members of the Society, under the direction of Alfred Fairbank, have worked on this project.

The English scribe is often called upon to produce work where the calligraphy, although an essential component, must be allied to decoration of a specific character and several disparate items may have to be included in the design. The challenge to the scribe in such a case is to reconcile fluency of writing with precision and finish in the decoration and also give unity to the whole work. The fluent calligraphy and sensitive touch of Irene Wellington and Joan Pilsbury, and the variety and precision of Dorothy Mahoney's writing are well known and admired. Heraldry has become increasingly popular, and among the scribes who combine sound heraldic designs with calligraphy are Ida Henstock, T. W. Swindlehurst and William Gardner.

In the forty years since the foundation of the Society there have been unparalleled changes in both aesthetic and economic spheres but it is remarkable that throughout these vast upheavals members of the Society have kept 'the noiseless tenor of their way'. The prestige of the Society has increased and it is now one of the five major craft societies represented in the Crafts Centre of Great Britain. Between the two World Wars the pressures of mass production might have been expected to crush the calligraphic revival, but the vitality of this small body of craftsmen has been sufficient to ensure its vigorous survival.

It might have been expected that English calligraphers would be called upon by type-founders and printers to a much larger extent than has occurred, and the reasons for this not being so are various and obscure. One obvious reason is that the type of work the professional English calligrapher performs is related to hand-craftsmanship and the making of individual works rather than to reproduction. However, some versatile scribes, such as John Woodcock, Ann Camp, Sheila Waters and Wendy Westover are successfully designing book jackets, book-plates, maps and similar works for reproduction.

The hands used by scribes in Great Britain today reflect the teaching of Edward Johnston, and formal writing tends towards a compressed version of the Foundational Hand; a set italic is also used extensively. Parallel with the trend on the Continent, the Uncial letter is being newly revived, and a contemporary version of the clear, open Carolingian script is used, which may indicate that alphabets based on the round O are finding favour again and counterbalancing the popularity of the elliptical letters.

Although no definite school of illumination has emerged, decoration is used extensively by English scribes and some have developed a personal style of illumination in their work. The modern trends in graphic arts today have not had as much influence on the decoration of the written page as in other fields.

Present Practice on the Continent

GERMANY AND SWITZERLAND: Lettering and typographic design were the first to benefit by the surge of interest in craftsmanship which, coming from William Morris and his circle, swept over Europe in the early years of this century. In Germany the movement was led by such men as Otto Echmann, Rudolf Koch, Fritz Helmuth Ehmcke, Walter Tiemann and Emil Weiss, and it was encouraged in the art schools.

The fine tradition of penmanship today is further enriched by craftsmen working in Germany and Switzerland, many of whom combine calligraphy with book design and typography, uniting all three in a satisfying relationship. After the advent of printing, books ceased to be written by hand, but formal writing and informal handwriting continued side by side with typography, only with diminished status. Most creative calligraphers and typographers today share the view that writing and type design are complementary to one another, having different purposes but constantly interacting on each other, and this is probably most clearly shown in the work of calligraphers and typographers on the Continent.

Jan Tschichold has exerted a considerable influence on book design in Europe and America. He studied at the Akademie für Graphische Kunst und Buchgewerbe in Leipzig and in Dresden, and later taught lettering and typography in Munich. Among his many publications are *An Illustrated History of Writing and Lettering*, an English edition of his *Geschichte der Schrift in Bildern* published in 1946, and his more extensive book containing numerous examples of calligraphy, printing and type faces, *Meisterbuch der Schrift* (Ravensburg, 1952).

Imre Reiner studied graphic art under Ernst Schneidler in Stuttgart and he is well known for his lively calligraphic inventions and his type designs. Max Caflisch was a pupil of both Jan Tschichold and Imre Reiner. He studied calligraphy and typography in Basle, where he later lectured on these subjects at the Allegemeine Gewerbeschule. He is a freelance consultant to various publishing firms and teaches at the School of Art at Zürich. He designed the Columna type face.

Walter Kaech who is a graphic artist living in Zürich has produced comprehensive books on calligraphy, lettering and typography, the latest being *Rhythm and Proportion in Lettering*, published in Switzerland in 1956.

Hermann Zapf was self-taught and influenced by the books of Edward Johnston and Rudolf Koch. He has written manuscripts in formal hands, taught lettering at the Werkkunstschule in Offenbach and lectured in Sweden and America. The type faces he has designed include Palatino, Melior and Optima. His well-known book *Feder und Stichel* (Pen and Graver) contains many splendid examples of his calligraphy and lettering engraved by August Rosenberger.

Following the precedent of German typography, scribes have tended to turn away from the traditional Gothic hand, with its angular, broken letters, to the use of Uncials and a formal italic which is clear and dignified, while retaining the rich colour and strong patterning associated with the Gothic styles.

CZECHOSLOVAKIA: The calligraphy of Oldřich Menhart of Prague is little known in England. Born in 1897, descended from a line of craftsmen, his early training made him a

OLDŘICH MENHART
Bookplate

master of pen and graver; he successfully combined calligraphy, lettering, typography and type design. He died in 1962.

Menhart absorbed the heritage of Western scripts and disciplined his hand by arduous practice; his penmanship has a vigorous quality, his letter-forms a rugged strength. He held that a good type cannot be designed until it has been written, and the pen has been the inspiration of his many type designs. One of Menhart's most remarkable works was writing out *Kytice*, a Czech classic, as a manuscript of some 150 pages; it was illustrated by Antonin Prochazka and the whole was reproduced facsimile by Method Kalab, in Prague, in 1940. The lettering Menhart used for the book became his Manuscript type, both roman and italic. Menhart said of his Uncial type, which appeared in 1949, that it was the result of twenty-six years of study of these handsome letters.

JAN VAN
KRIMPEN
Monogram

THE NETHERLANDS: The Dutch were fortunate in having such a skilled and far-sighted craftsman as Jan van Krimpen at the time when the traditional Gothic types were being displaced by roman and italic founts. Van Krimpen was a calligrapher and a typographer and a man of wide vision. The success of his printing types, chiefly designed for the firm of Joh. Enschedé en Zonen, brought him requests for lettering of many kinds, written, painted, and engraved. He wrote a number of manuscripts on vellum for his own pleasure and instruction. His formal calligraphy, which included work presented to royalty, helped to develop the qualities that are of most value in type design, and he believed calligraphy to be a fundamental training for the student.

Chris Brand, also a calligrapher and typographer, was self-taught with the aid of Johnston's manual. He writes the formal hands and teaches calligraphy, lettering and typography in Breda, 's Hertogenbosch and Tilburg. He has done a great deal to encourage the use of fine handwriting in the Netherlands. In association with Ben Engelhart he has produced several works on handwriting, including a writing method for primary schools in a delightful series of booklets called *Ritmisch Schrijven*.

CHRIS BRAND
*Monogram for a
publisher*

SWEDEN AND DENMARK: The work of Erik Lindegren and Bent Rohde, both illustrated in this book, deserve special attention for the beauty of their italic hands.

THE U.S.S.R.: In the Soviet Union craftsmen do not use the edged-pen at present; letters are either drawn or painted. There is more interest in writing in the Baltic Republics where the Latin alphabet is used. The most successful craftsmen are the Estonian scribes who work in Tallinn. Villu Toots, whose work is illustrated here, published his first book *Tänapäeva kiri* (Lettering of Today) in 1956; it shows a method of writing with the edged-pen. His second book *300 Burtu Veidi* (300 Alphabets) was published by the Latvian State Republic in 1960. Exhibitions of lettering were held in Moscow in 1953 and 1961, and a

book by Villu Toots, *The Art of Writing and Lettering*, based on the methods of Edward Johnston, will be published in Moscow shortly by Iskusstvo, and it is hoped it will arouse an interest in calligraphy in Russia.

ITALY AND OTHER LATIN COUNTRIES: Included in the illustrations is an item of calligraphy by Adrian Frutiger, the type designer who works in Paris. It is disappointing that Italy, the country from which our Roman alphabet derives, and which still displays the Roman letters in all their beauty of classical perfection, should not have produced any contemporary professional calligraphers of standing, so far as we know.

Present Practice in America

The growth of interest in calligraphy in America has tended to emerge and flourish round the teaching and work of individual calligraphers in various centres, in particular in New York, Rhode Island, Boston, Chicago and Portland.

One of the earliest exponents of formal writing was the late Ernst Detterer of Newberry Library, Chicago. He came to England in 1913 and for a short time had private lessons from Edward Johnston. He has played an important part in the development of the calligraphic tradition in America, particularly in the Mid-west, by his teaching and practice of the craft. He inspired such distinguished scribes as James Hayes and Raymond F. Da Boll to broaden the uses of calligraphy and carry on his tradition of craftsmanship after his death in 1947.

James Hayes became interested in penmanship at an early age and in 1926 decided to attend the school of the Art Institute in Chicago; the printing arts course had a class in writing at that time, as a basis for the study of typography. This was the only class in the Mid-west where calligraphy was taught in the Johnston tradition. After studying for three years with Detterer, he gained valuable experience in display work, and since 1940 he has been freelancing in calligraphy and lettering; his work covers a wide range, from designing diplomas and awards to memorials, presentations and book-plates. Most of his work is original and a small proportion only is designed for reproduction.

W. A. Dwiggins, who died in 1947, had a designing talent unique in the graphic arts of America. As a calligrapher he used a formal and semi-formal hand, first in advertising and then in book production; his work for type design was outstanding. As early as 1907 he suggested to Goudy that they should form a calligraphic society, but in vain. In 1925 he formed an imaginary 'Society of Calligraphers' as a hoax and issued handsome certificates to twenty-two honorary members, receiving as a result many enquiries from the unwary.

Dwiggins showed an innate sense of design in all his work; his writing owes nothing to European sources and it has gaiety and originality of its own. Mr Philip Hofer said in 1935 'that the revival of interest in this art today is in large measure due to him. In it he stands head and shoulders above any other American designer—as individual in his style as he is accomplished and imaginative.'

John Howard Benson, who was born in 1901 and died in 1956, lived and worked in Rhode Island. He studied in New York at the Art Student League at a time when lettering had no formal place in art education. He was given a copy of Johnston's manual and it inspired in him such a desire to create beautiful letters that his life became directed to this end. He was a genuine and versatile craftsman. Typography attracted him, but a chance event changed the direction of his work and he turned to cutting letters of beauty and distinction in stone. As an outcome of his teaching and practice he wrote, together with his partner Graham Carey, a manual for the student, *Elements of Lettering*. Benson owned an Arrighi manual of 1533 which he translated and having mastered the italic hand for his own use, he transcribed *La Operina* and in 1954 it was published. It was an immediate and outstanding success, bringing him many new friends towards the end of his life.

George Salter, a notable calligrapher himself, and an inspiring teacher at the Cooper Union Art School in New York for many years, has brought to calligraphy a new spontaneity. He has trained a generation of scribes whose talents have been rapidly appreciated by publishing and commerce. His own enjoyment in calligraphy is revealed in his book jackets.

Philip Grushkin is also a product of the Cooper Union Art School, having studied under George Salter, and for the past fifteen years he has been teaching calligraphy, lettering and illustrating there. He finds a lot of pleasure himself in calligraphy.

Arnold Bank, who is well known for his book jackets and titles, attracts large numbers of students to his lively classes, and his own calligraphic designs are as dynamic as his teaching.

Interest in the revival of italic handwriting began in the first quarter of this century in America; Ernst Detterer was teaching italic in 1924. Frederic Warde contributed to the revival by publishing in 1926 a facsimile edition of Arrighi's two writing manuals. Much credit is due to Paul Standard who, as a practising calligrapher himself, has been teaching italic in Boston and New York. He seeks a reform of handwriting in American schools based on Arrighi's italic hand and the English exemplars. In the West the teaching of Professor Lloyd Reynolds is evident.

Both a set italic hand and more freely written versions are used extensively by American calligraphers in their book jackets, titles, certificates and other similar works, especially those designed for reproduction. The outstanding impression of the work of American scribes is the gaiety and freedom of penmanship, allied to an emphasis on creative spontaneity which is perhaps to be expected from their ebullient and vital society; enjoyment in the use of the edged⁄pen is communicated in their writing. The formal hands do not appear to exert the same appeal in America as in Britain where the influence of Edward Johnston is still strong.

The Elements of Calligraphy

PHILIP GRUSHKIN
Trademark for Albert D. Smith & Co., book cloth manufacturers, New York

An appreciation of the elements of calligraphy and a knowledge of the technique of the craft are of first importance. The form and construction of letters can only be properly understood by using the tools of the craft. The metal edged⁄pens which are used extensively today are generally inferior to well⁄prepared quills, which remain the best instruments for formal writing, but they are now difficult to obtain. Metal edged⁄pens, both straight and oblique, are made in a wide range of sizes for right⁄ and left⁄handed calligraphers, and they must be kept sharp and clean if they are to make crisp strokes. Inks must flow easily without clogging in the pen, and a good soluble carbon ink is the best in this respect. Waterproof inks are too thick and gummy to flow easily. Good quality paper with an unglazed surface makes a suitable writing material for ordinary use. If the paper is too smooth the pen will slide over the surface uncomfortably; if too rough the freedom of the pen is in danger, and if too porous the ink tends to feather and spread. Well⁄prepared vellum gives the perfect writing surface for the practised scribe. All who want to acquire a formal hand have the advantage of one of the most comprehensive handbooks ever compiled for craftsmen in Edward Johnston's *Writing & Illuminating, & Lettering*, published in 1906, and *The Calligrapher's Handbook*, published in 1951, is a useful sequel.

In analysing a formal hand, whether an historical or contemporary example, the following points should be observed: the general appearance of the page, the pattern of the lines of writing, whether delicate or strong in texture, and the secondary pattern made by the ascending and descending strokes, sometimes flourished, in the spaces between the close⁄ patterned lines of the bodies of the letters. The relative proportions of text and margins to page should be noted. The method of spacing the lines is interesting; note whether they are ruled in a block of lines of equal length (as for prose), in columns (for lists of names), or in lines of unequal length (for poetry). The style of writing will depend on the pen stroke, which is the relative unit for the letter; the average height and weight of a Minuscule letter is four⁄and⁄ a⁄half nib widths. The O is the key letter of the alphabet in formal writing; note whether it is round, compressed, angular, or elliptical in shape. Are the letters upright or sloping, joined or separate? Are the thin strokes horizontal or oblique, and what is the angle of the thin stroke to the horizontal line? Does the script give the impression of strength and stability, elegance and movement, richness or delicacy?

31

An appreciation of penmanship is enhanced by an understanding of the elements involved in producing a beautiful piece of writing. The calligrapher is concerned to write fluent and legible letters, in spacing them well in the words and lines and in arranging them on the page. The spaces inside the letters (the counters) are as important as the spaces between the letters and words. The ability to space well comes by practice; the experienced calligrapher spaces by eye. The trained eye has the ability to recognise whether a script is good; the analysis of fine examples of writing will develop taste.

Edward Johnston taught that the *desirable* qualities of good writing are: *Legibility, Beauty, Character*. The *essential* qualities: *Simplicity, Distinctiveness, Proportion*. The qualities of formal penmanship: *Unity, Sharpness, Freedom*.

Legibility is of first importance and it is a quality difficult to define. Robert Bridges held that 'True legibility consists in the *certainty of deciphering* and that depends not on what any one reader may be accustomed to, nor even on the use of customary forms, but rather on the consistent and accurate formation of the letters.' Each letter has distinct characteristics of its own, but all letters in an alphabet should have a family likeness which makes for unity. Contrasts in size of writing, styles of writing, in colour and in decoration, add interest and liveliness to the page, but they should add and not distract from the unity of the whole. The fundamental construction of letters, their proportions and their derivation, must be understood, as these give letters their characteristic shapes. Legibility will to a large extent depend on the unity and rhythm in the writing, and these qualities come with knowledge and practice. Rhythm and proportion together make for unity and distinctiveness.

Johnston's third triad: *Unity, Sharpness, Freedom* is concerned with technique in formal writing. Sharpness results from a well-cut or sharpened pen writing on a well-prepared surface; as a result of these technical considerations the pen can be used freely with a sensitive touch to make fluent letters. Writing at the appropriate speed gives rhythm and vitality to the work; writing that is laboured will lack these qualities, however carefully each letter is formed in itself.

The first duty of the scribe is 'to the thought or image intended to be communicated by the Author' of the work being transcribed. The thinking and planning must be done before the writing begins. If the scribe is hampered by technical considerations, or consciously seeks to display his own skill, the work will have neither simplicity nor distinctiveness. Beauty may come as a bonus or reward for right methods of penmanship.

Frederic Warde held that 'Calligraphy may be defined as the writing of a person who has trained his hand, his eye and his judgment to write habitually according to a rational method. . . . Calligraphy is most admirable and interesting when it has been done according to its classic rules. . . . The rules aimed at one objective—FORM. . . . Real style is impossible without form.'

The Choice of Illustrations

PAGES 34–48   FROM THE BEGINNING OF THE REVIVAL TO 1940

In this section the illustrations have been chosen to outline the tradition of calligraphy in Britain, the Continent and America, from the first days of the revival until the outbreak of the Second World War. They begin with a page written by the pioneer William Morris, in an italic hand. The selection of writing by Edward Johnston is chosen to illustrate various hands founded on traditional styles, as these were the basis of his teaching. The advertisement for Sun Engraving was an unusual project for Johnston to have carried out, as he seldom worked for reproduction. Examples of the work of Graily Hewitt and founder members of the Society of Scribes and Illuminators follow. Work by Rudolf von Larisch, Rudolf Koch and Anna Simons on the Continent, and W. A. Dwiggins and Ernst Detterer in America complete the survey of this period.

PAGES 48–71   EXAMPLES OF ORIGINAL CALLIGRAPHY, 1941 TO 1961

Examples have been chosen of formal calligraphy used in illuminated addresses, rolls of honour, manuscript books and similar productions. These are unique works, usually carried out on vellum, most of them have been written by members of the Society of Scribes and Illuminators, who are professional calligraphers and specialists in this field.

PAGES 72–87   CALLIGRAPHY FOR REPRODUCTION, 1941 TO 1961

The scribe who designs for reproduction today has room to exercise a lively invention. The book jackets, titles, book-plates, certificates, greetings cards and posters, included in these illustrations, give some idea of the scope and variety. In designing calligraphy for printing the approach is obviously different from that of making an original manuscript. The various methods of reproduction must be fully grasped if crisp and distinguished work is to be produced.

PAGES 88–95   MODEL HANDS AND EXEMPLARS AS AIDS TO TEACHING

Many professional calligraphers combine teaching with their written work, which often impels them to make exemplars and copy-books for the use of their students. Illustrations of a few of these invaluable aids to teaching are included. They follow in the steps of Ludovico degli Arrighi whose first copy-book *La Operina* appeared in Rome in 1522, a page of which is reproduced here.

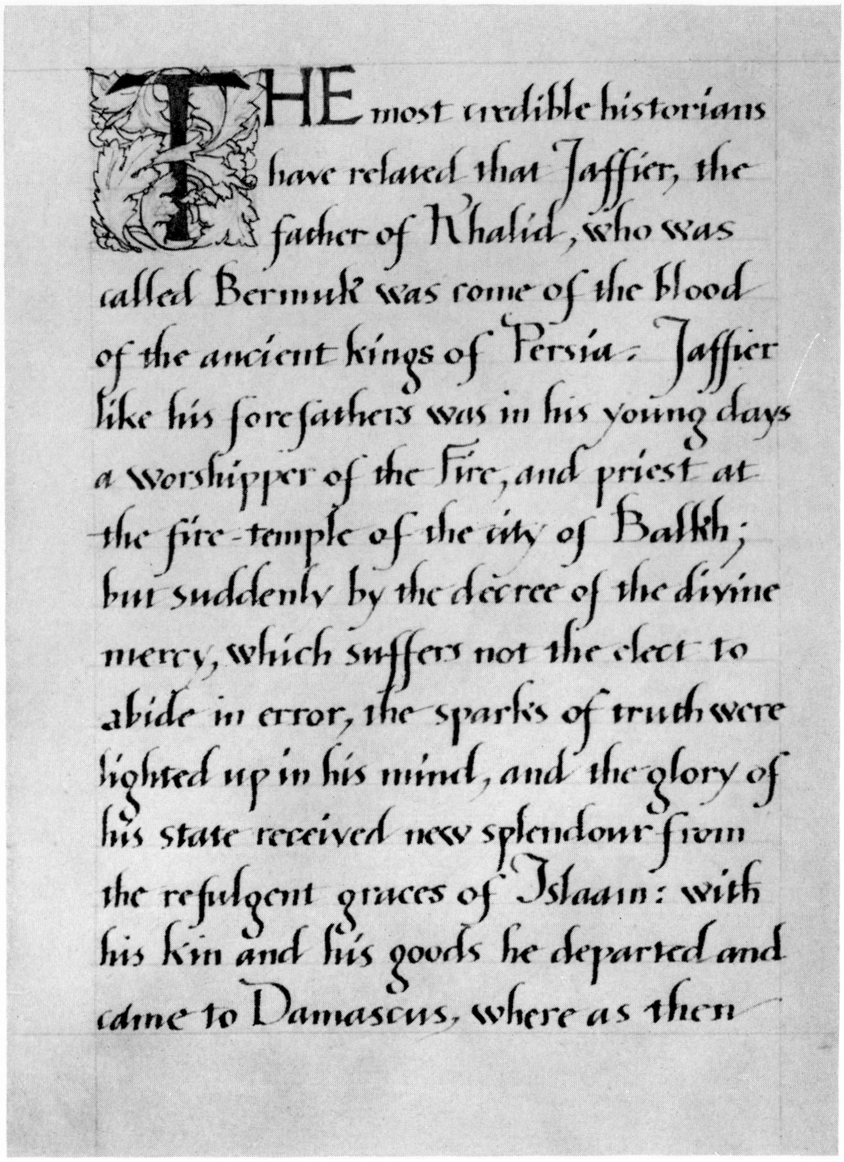

THE most credible historians have related that Jaffier, the father of Khalid, who was called Bermuk was come of the blood of the ancient kings of Persia. Jaffier like his forefathers was in his young days a worshipper of the fire, and priest at the fire-temple of the city of Balkh; but suddenly by the decree of the divine mercy, which suffers not the elect to abide in error, the sparks of truth were lighted up in his mind, and the glory of his state received new splendour from the refulgent graces of Islaam: with his kin and his goods he departed and came to Damascus, where as then

WILLIAM MORRIS
Page for a manuscript book.
Bodleian Library. (Reduced)

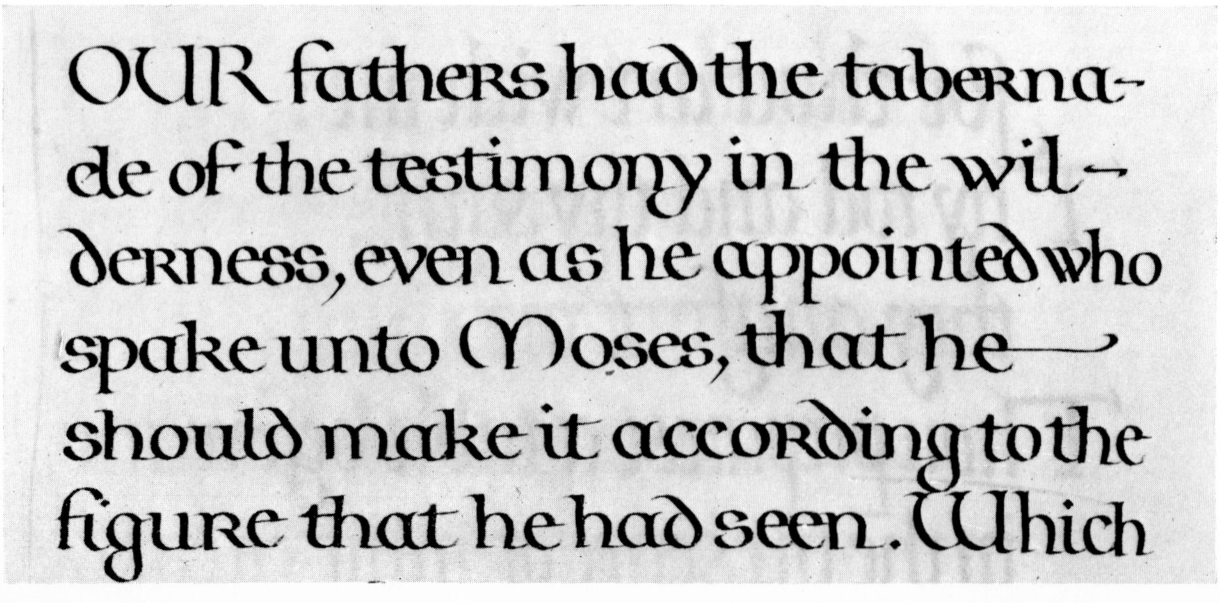

EDWARD JOHNSTON
Part of a page from
A Book of Sample Scripts
made for Sir Sydney Cockerell,
completed in March 1914. Written in
a Half Uncial hand with Uncials
to match. Victoria and Albert
Museum (L. 4391–1959).
(Size 9 in. × 7 in.)

OUR fathers had the taberna-cle of the testimony in the wil-derness, even as he appointed who spake unto Moses, that he should make it according to the figure that he had seen. Which

EDWARD JOHNSTON
Page from
A Book of Sample Scripts
*written in a small roman hand, the
first four lines in red. Victoria
and Albert Museum (L. 4391–1959).
(Size 9 in. × 7 in.)*

EDWARD JOHNSTON
*Opening from a book of his own
verses made for his wife. Written in
black and red in 1918. By courtesy of
Miss Priscilla Johnston.
(Slightly reduced)*

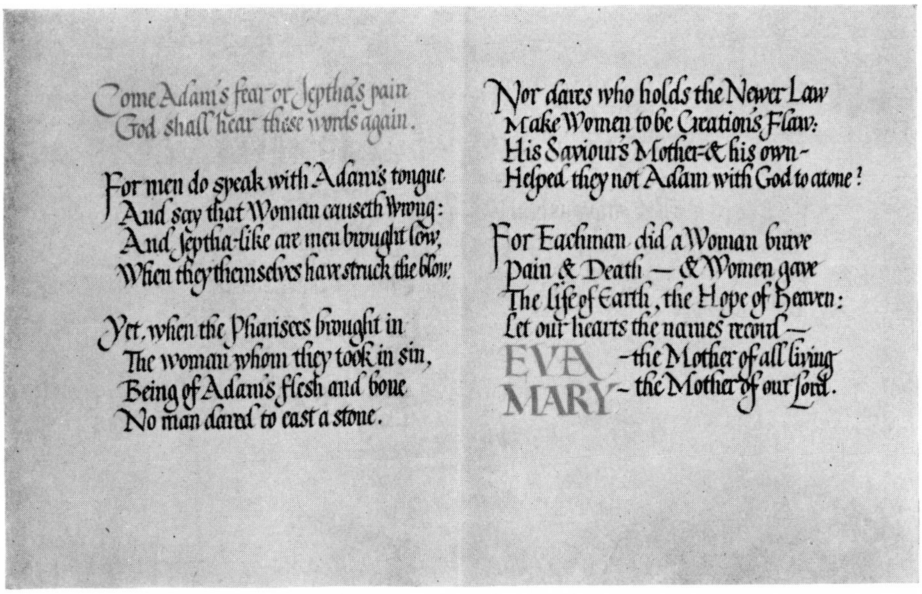

Dignus es, Domine Deus noster, acci-
pere gloriam, et honorem, et virtutem:
quia tu creasti omnia, et propter vo-
luntatem tuam erant, et creata sunt.
And I saw in the right hand of
him that sat on the throne a
book written within and on the
back, close sealed with seven
seals. And I saw a strong angel
proclaiming with a great voice,
Who is worthy to open the book,
and to loose the seals thereof?
And no one in the heaven, or on

Come Adam's fear or Jeptha's pain
God shall hear these words again.

For men do speak with Adam's tongue
And say that Woman causeth Wrong:
And Jeptha-like are men brought low,
When they themselves have struck the blow;

Yet, when the Pharisees brought in
The woman whom they took in sin,
Being of Adam's flesh and bone
No man dared to cast a stone.

Nor dares who holds the Newer Law
Make Women to be Creation's Flaw:
His Saviour's Mother & his own—
Helped they not Adam with God to atone?

For Eachman did a Woman brave
Pain & Death — & Women gave
The life of Earth, the Hope of Heaven:
Let our hearts the names record —
EVA —the Mother of all living
MARY ~ the Mother of our Lord.

Et haec scribimus
vobis ut gaudeatis,
et gaudium ves‑
trum sit plenum.
Et haec est annunciatio, quam
audivimus ab eo, et annunciamus
vobis: Quoniam Deus lux est,
& tenebrae in eo non sunt ullae.

Note: This copy is written with a pen, not printed. EJ 5 Feb. 1918 A.D.

In order that a child may learn how to write well the teaching of handwriting should begin with the practice of a Formal Hand. This Manuscript is written with a BROAD-NIBBED PEN which makes the strokes thick or thin according to the direction in which it moves. The strokes are generally begun downwards or forwards & the letters are formed of several strokes *(the pen being lifted after each stroke):* thus *c* consists of *two* strokes, the first a long curve down, the second a short curve forward. The triangular 'heads' *(as for b or d)* are made by *three* strokes; 1st. a short thick curve down, 2nd. a short thin stroke up *(the nib for this stroke being placed on the beginning of the first and slid up to the right)*, 3rd. the thick straight *stem* stroke of the letter itself down *(the pen for this stroke not being lifted).*

Broad-nibbed steel pens and Reeds may be used: Quill pens are very good but require special cutting. How to cut Quill and Reed pens may be learned from my Handbook "Writing & Illuminating, & Lettering" *(John Hogg, London: 6s. 6d. net)* besides how to make MS. Books and to write in colour. Edward Johnston: ' Ditchling, Sussex.

THIS SHEET IS PUBLISHED BY DOUGLAS PEPLER at HAMPSHIRE HOUSE HAMMERSMITH 1916 A.D.

Price 4/‑

EDWARD JOHNSTON
The first four lines written in his Foundational hand, and the four lines in formal italics below are scripts developed from Edward Johnston's study of the 10th-century MS. indicated on page 13. The printing is in red and includes a wood-block of lettering by Eric Gill. One of four Writing Sheets published by Douglas Pepler. By courtesy of Miss Priscilla Johnston.
(Size 11¼ in. × 8¾ in.)

EDWARD JOHNSTON
Advertisement in The Times, *Printing Number 29th October 1929. Written in a pointed formal italic hand.*
(Size 5¾ in. × 8 in.)

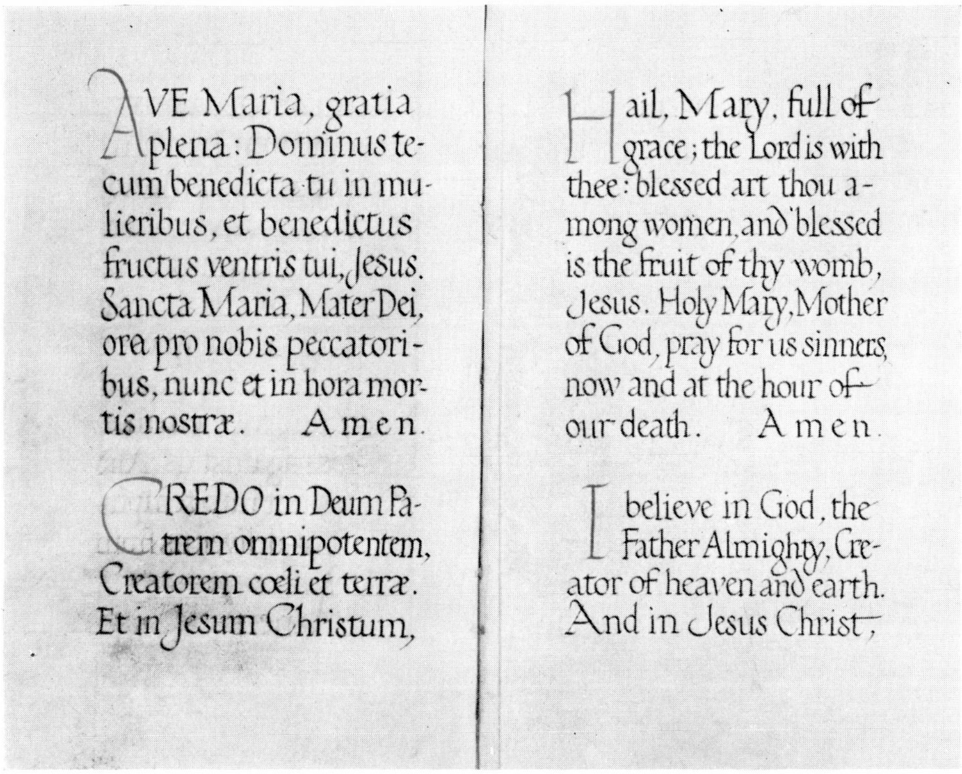

AVE Maria, gratia plena: Dominus tecum benedicta tu in mulieribus, et benedictus fructus ventris tui, Jesus. Sancta Maria, Mater Dei, ora pro nobis peccatoribus, nunc et in hora mortis nostræ. Amen.

CREDO in Deum Patrem omnipotentem, Creatorem cœli et terræ. Et in Jesum Christum,

Hail, Mary, full of grace; the Lord is with thee: blessed art thou among women, and blessed is the fruit of thy womb, Jesus. Holy Mary, Mother of God, pray for us sinners, now and at the hour of our death. Amen.

I believe in God, the Father Almighty, Creator of heaven and earth. And in Jesus Christ,

EDWARD JOHNSTON
Opening from a book of Prayers written in a roman hand, made for Eric Gill. In the possession of Heather Child.
(Size 5 in. × 3 in.)

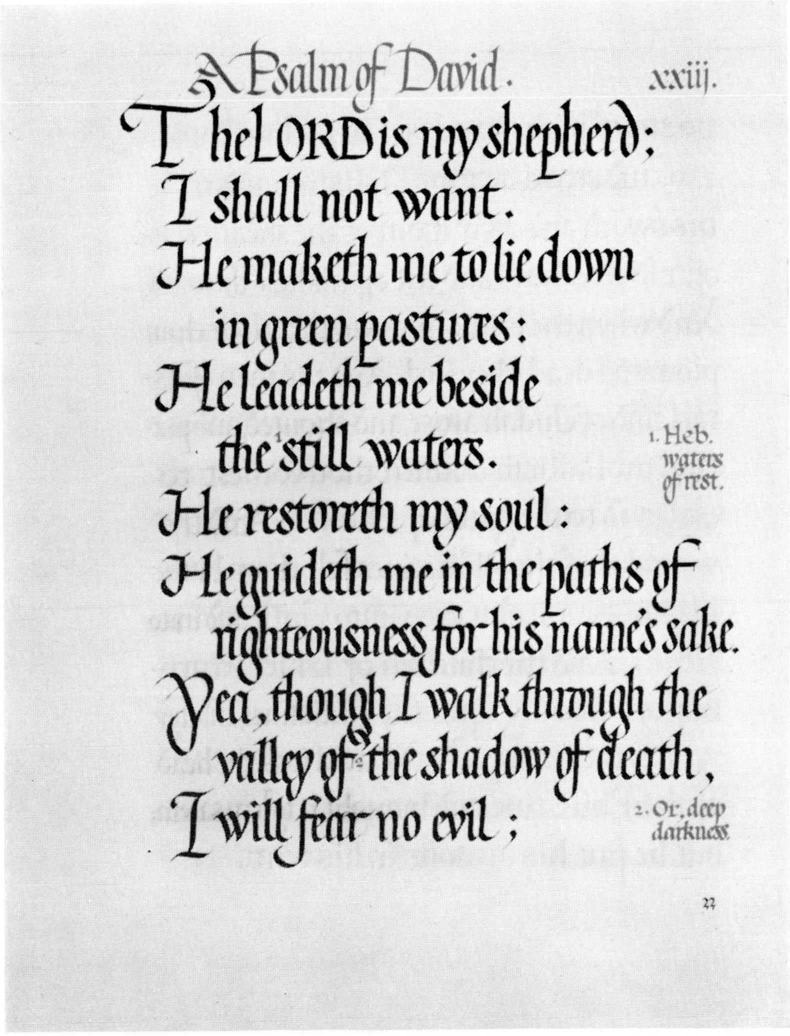

EDWARD JOHNSTON
Page from
A Book of Sample Scripts,
written in a formal italic hand with title and notes in red. Victoria and Albert Museum (L. 4391-1959).
(Size 9 in. × 7 in.)

A Psalm of David.   xxiij.

The LORD is my shepherd;
I shall not want.
He maketh me to lie down
    in green pastures:
He leadeth me beside
    the still waters.
He restoreth my soul:
He guideth me in the paths of
    righteousness for his name's sake.
Yea, though I walk through the
    valley of the shadow of death,
I will fear no evil;

1. Heb.
waters
of rest.

2. Or, deep
darkness

22

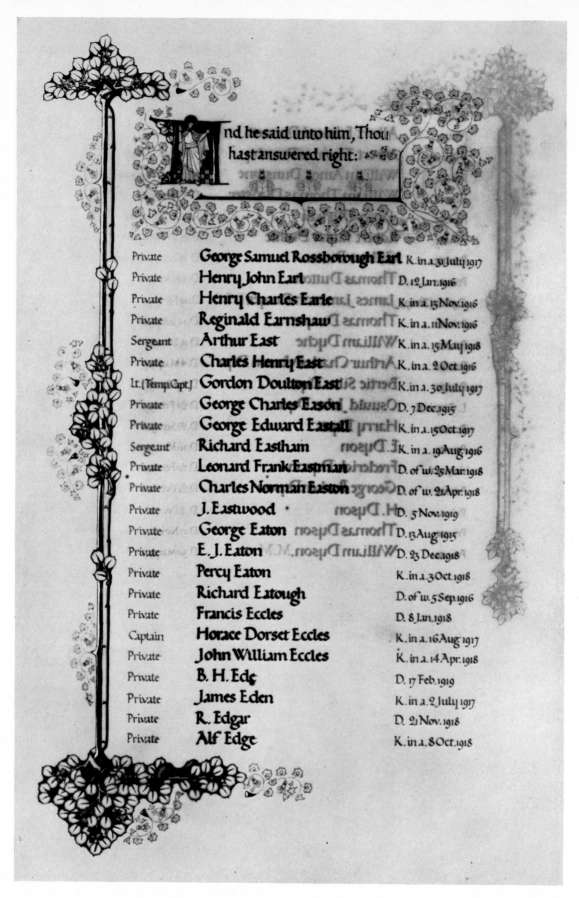

And he said unto him, Thou hast answered right:

Private	George Samuel Rossborough Earl	K. in a. 31 July. 1917
Private	Henry John Earl	D. 12 Jan. 1916
Private	Henry Charles Earle	K. in a. 13 Nov. 1916
Private	Reginald Earnshaw	K. in a. 11 Nov. 1916
Sergeant	Arthur East	K. in a. 15 May. 1918
Private	Charles Henry East	K. in a. 2 Oct. 1916
Lt. (Temp. Capt.)	Gordon Doulton East	K. in a. 30 July. 1917
Private	George Charles Eason	D. 7 Dec. 1915
Private	George Edward Eastall	K. in a. 15 Oct. 1917
Sergeant	Richard Eastham	K. in a. 19 Aug. 1916
Private	Leonard Frank Eastman	D. of w. 25 Mar. 1918
Private	Charles Norman Easton	D. of w. 21 Apr. 1918
Private	J. Eastwood	D. 5 Nov. 1919
Private	George Eaton	D. 13 Aug. 1915
Private	E. J. Eaton	D. 23 Dec. 1918
Private	Percy Eaton	K. in a. 3 Oct. 1918
Private	Richard Eatough	D. of w. 5 Sep. 1916
Private	Francis Eccles	D. 8 Jan. 1918
Captain	Horace Dorset Eccles	K. in a. 16 Aug. 1917
Private	John William Eccles	K. in a. 14 Apr. 1918
Private	B. H. Edge	D. 17 Feb. 1919
Private	James Eden	K. in a. 2 July. 1917
Private	R. Edgar	D. 21 Nov. 1918
Private	Alf Edge	K. in a. 8 Oct. 1918

MEMORIAL ROLL OF THE ROYAL ARMY MEDICAL CORPS · *The work of* GRAILY HEWITT *and his assistants Horace Higgins, Madelyn Walker, Florence Raymond, Ida Henstock, Vera Peacock and Reco Capey. The writing, in a 15th-century Italian style, is mainly the work of Horace Higgins. In the Chapter House Westminster Abbey. By courtesy of the Director General, Army Medical Services. (Reduced)*

GꝟRI

HE whom this scroll commemorates was numbered among those who, at the call of King and Country, left all that was dear to them, endured hardness, faced danger, and finally passed out of the sight of men by the path of duty and self-sacrifice, giving up their own lives that others might live in freedom.

Let those who come after see to it that his name be not forgotten.

GRAILY HEWITT
Scroll sent from H.M. King George V to relatives of the fallen after the First World War. Engraved by Noel Rooke. Reproduced in black with capital letter in red and shield in colour.
(Size 11 in. × 7¼ in.)

RUDOLF von LARISCH
A tribute to Anna Simons in gratitude for her work as a teacher, artist and pioneer, in the form of a certificate. (Reduced)

FRAU PROFESSOR
ANNA SIMONS
sie erfolgreiche Gestalterin in der Buch- und Schreib-
kunst hat nicht nur zahlreiche künstlerische Arbeiten
geschaffen, sie hat auch durch ihr langjähriges päda-
gogisches Wirken auf dem Gebiete der Schriftgestal-
tung neue Jünger und Anhänger gewonnen. Ich
freue mich, als ihr Kollege und Mitstrebender dieser
hervorragenden Leistungen und bringe ihr aus die-
sem Anlasse meine herzlichsten Glückwünsche und
Grüße in alter Freundschaft und Ergebenheit.

Wien, im Nov. 1932   Prof. Rudolf von Larisch

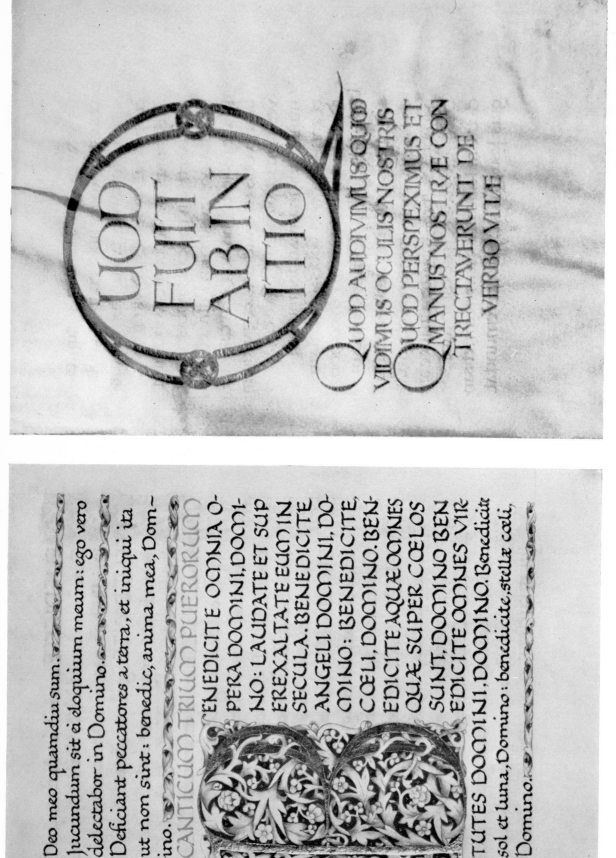

ERNEST TREGLOWN
*Recto page from a manuscript book. By
courtesy of Charles Thomas Esq.*
(Reduced)

LOUISE POWELL
*Recto page from a manuscript book of
Psalms. Written in
black and vermilion with initial letter in
burnished gold. Victoria and Albert
Museum (L. 4393–1930). (Reduced)*

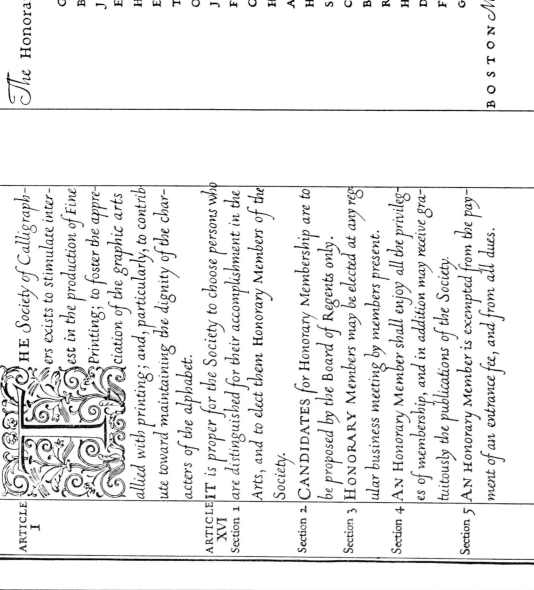

ARTICLE I

THE Society of Calligraphers exists to stimulate interest in the production of Fine Printing; to foster the appreciation of the graphic arts allied with printing; and, particularly, to contribute toward maintaining the dignity of the characters of the alphabet.

ARTICLE XVI

IT is proper for the Society to choose persons who are distinguished for their accomplishment in the Arts, and to elect them Honorary Members of the Society.

Section 1

Section 2 CANDIDATES for Honorary Membership are to be proposed by the Board of Regents only.

Section 3 HONORARY Members may be elected at any regular business meeting by members present.

Section 4 AN Honorary Member shall enjoy all the privileges of membership, and in addition may receive gratuitously the publications of the Society.

Section 5 AN Honorary Member is exempted from the payment of an entrance fee, and from all dues.

The Honorary Members of the Society:

GEORGE G. ADOMEIT
BEATRICE L. BECKER
JOHN BIANCHI
EDGAR SUMNER BLISS
HENRY LEWIS BULLEN
EARNEST ELMO CALKINS
THOMAS MAITLAND CLELAND
OSWALD BRUCE COOPER
JOHN COTTON DANA
FREDERIC W. GOUDY
CHARLES HOPKINSON
HENRY LEWIS JOHNSON
ALFRED A. KNOPF
HENRY W. KENT
STANLEY MORISON
CARL PURINGTON ROLLINS
BRUCE ROGERS
RUDOLPH RUZICKA
HENRY H. TAYLOR
DANIEL BERKELEY UPDIKE
FRANK WEITENKAMPF
GEORGE PARKER WINSHIP

BOSTON May 11th 1925

W. A. DWIGGINS · The Honorary Members of the Society of Calligraphers.
11th May 1925. Printed in black ink on Japanese paper. (Size $9\frac{3}{4}$ in. × $7\frac{1}{2}$ in.)

GESCHICHTE DER SCHRIFT

GRIECHISCHE·KAPITALSCHRIFT·III·JAHRHUNDERT·v·CHRISTI

ΕΠΙΣΤΟΛΑΣΥΠΟΑΓΗΣΑΡΧΟΥΕΝΑΣΥΓΕΡΜΕΝΙΑΙΟΓ
ΚΑΙΤΑΣΓΕΡΙΤΟΚΑΡΙΟΝΧΩΡΑΣΟΥΘΕΙΣΑΜΦΕΣΒΑΤΕΙ
ΤΟΝΡΟΔΙΩΝΕΓΚΛΑΟΥΝΤΑΣΟΤΙΧΩΡΑΣΤΕΓΛΗ

BYZANTINISCHE SCHRIFT·PAPYRUS·III JAHRHUNDERT·n·CHRISTI

ΕΚΤΟΡΑΔΑΚΡΥΧΕΟΝΤΕΣΟΔΥΡΟΝΤΟΠΡΟΠΥΛΩΝ
ΕΙΝΗΑΡΕΚΑΙΦΡΟΙΟΓΕΡΩΝΛΑΟΙΣΙ ΜΕΤΗΥΔΑ·
ΕΙΣΑΤΕΜΟΙΟΥΡΕΥΣΙΔΙΕΛΘΕΜΕΝΑΥΤΑΡΕΠΕΙΤΑ
ΑCΕCΘΕΚΛΑΥΘΜΟΙΟΕΠΤΗΝΑΓΑΓΩΜΙΔΟΜΟΝΔΟ

RÖMISCHE·KAPITALSCHRIFT·IV·JAHRHUNDERT·n·CHRISTI

IPSEVOLANSTENVESSESVSTVLITALESADAVRAS
CVRRITITERTVTVMNONSETIVSAEQVORECLASSIS
PROMISSISQVEPATRISNEPTVNIINTERRITAFERITVR

UNZIALSCHRIFT·VI·JAHRHUNDERT·n·CHRISTI

INPRINCIPIOERATUERBUMETUERBUMERATAPUD
DEUMETDEUSERATUERBUMHOCERATINPRINCIP
IOAPUDDEUMOMNIAPERIPSUMFACTASUNTET

IRISCHE·HALBUNZIALSCHRIFT·VII·JAHRHUNDERT·n·CHRISTI

sine ipsum factum est nihil quod factum est
in ipso uita erat et uita erat lux hominum
et lux in tenebris lucet et tenebrae eam non
comprehenderunt fuit homo missus a Deo

Geschrieben von Anna Simons, München   Verlag Heintze & Blanckertz, Berlin-Leipzig

ANNA SIMONS
A specimen page from Die Geschichte der Schrift,
a portfolio of examples of handwriting from the 9th to the 16th century.
Verlag Heintze & Blanckertz, about 1930. (Reduced)

42

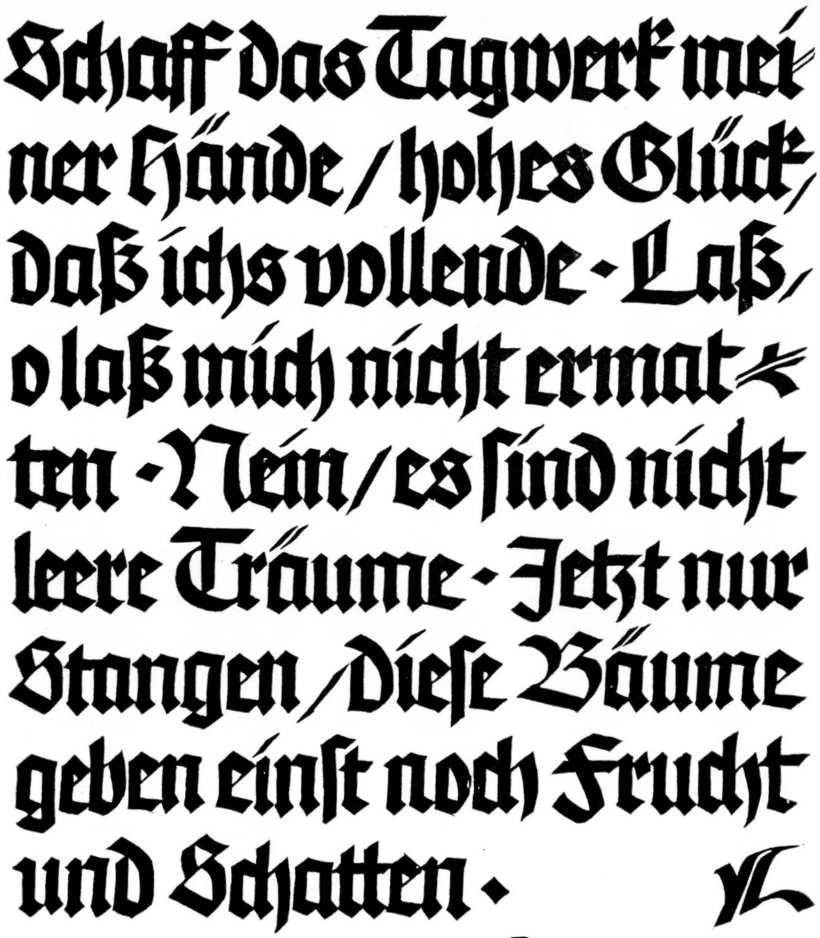

Schaff das Tagwerk mei
ner Hände / hohes Glück,
daß ichs vollende · Laß,
o laß mich nicht ermat-
ten · Nein / es sind nicht
leere Träume · Jetzt nur
Stangen / diese Bäume
geben einst noch Frucht
und Schatten ·   YL

Bild 21

RUDOLF KOCH
Illustration from Das Schreibbuchlein,
an introduction to writing with woodcuts by Fritz Kredel. 1935.
The pattern of the writing has been considered carefully as a whole.
Decorative inverted commas have been used as a space filling
device in the fourth and last line.
(Size 7 in. × 5½ in.)

RUDOLF KOCH
A Gothic hand more freely written than in the illustration
above but from the same source

Schaffe in mir Gott, ein reines Herze,
und gib mir einen neuen, gewissen Geist.
Verwirf mich nicht von deinem Angesicht
und nimm deinen heiligen Geist
nicht von mir.

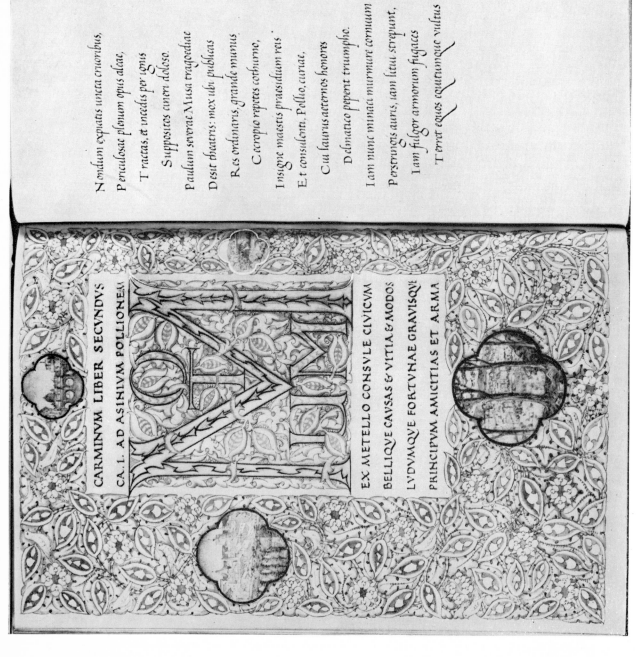

Nondum expiatis uncta cruoribus,
Periculosae plenum opus aleae,
Tractas, et incedis per ignis
Suppositos cineri doloso.

Paulum severae Musa tragoediae
Desit theatris: mox ubi publicas
Res ordinaris, grande munus
Cecropio repetes cothurno,

Insigne maestis praesidium reis
Et consulenti, Pollio, curiae,
Cui laurus aeternos honores
Delmatico peperit triumpho.

Iam nunc minaci murmure cornuum
Perstringis auris, iam litui strepunt,
Iam fulgor armorum fugaces
Terret equos equitumque vultus.

CARMINVM LIBER SECVNDVS
CA. I. AD ASINIVM POLLIONEM

EX METELLO CONSVLE CIVICVM
BELLIQVE CAVSAS & VITIA & MODOS
LVDVMQVE FORTVNAE GRAVISQVE
PRINCIPVM AMICITIAS ET ARMA

Horace: Odes and Epodes. *Writing and gilding by* ALFRED FAIRBANK,
illuminating by LOUISE POWELL, *1927 to 1931.*
By courtesy of Mrs St John Hornby.
(*Size 9 in × 6 in.*)

PELIACO quondam prognatae uertice pinus
Dicuntur liquidas Neptuni nasse per undas
Phasides ad fluctus et fines Aeetaeos,
Cum lecti iuuenes, Argiuae robora pubis,
Auratam optantes Colchis auertere pellem
Ausi sunt uada salsa cita decurrere puppi,
Caerula uerrentes abiegnis aequora palmis.
Diua quibus retinens in summis urbibus arces
Ipsa leui fecit uolitantem flamine currum,
Pinea coniungens inflexae texta carinae.
Illa rudem cursu prima imbuit Amphitriten.
Quae simul ac rostro uentosum proscidit aequor,
Tortaque remigio spumis incanuit unda,
Emersere feri candenti e gurgite uultus
Aequoreae monstrum Nereides admirantes.
Illa, atque haud alia, uiderunt luce marinas
Mortales oculi nudato corpore Nymphas

Nutricum tenus exstantes e gurgite cano
Tum Thetidis Peleus incensus fertur amore,
Tum Thetis humanos non despexit hymenaeos,
Tum Thetidi pater ipse iugandum Pelea sensit.
O nimis optato saeclorum tempore nati
Heroes, saluete, deum genus! o bona mater!
Vos ego saepe meo uos carmine compellabo.
Teque adeo eximie taedis felicibus aucte,
Thessaliae columen Peleu, cui Iuppiter ipse,
Ipse suos diuum genitor concessit amores;
Tene Thetis tenuit pulcerrima Neptunine?
Tene suam Tethys concessit ducere neptem,
Oceanusque, mari totum qui amplectitur orbem?
Quae simul optato finitae tempore luces
Aduenere, domum conuentu tota frequentat
Thessalia, oppletur laetanti regia coetu:
Dona ferunt prae se, declarant gaudia uultu.
Deseritur Scyros, linquunt Phthiotica Tempe,
Crannonisque domos ac moenia Larisaea,
Pharsaliam coeunt, Pharsalia tecta frequentant.

Opening from a manuscript copy of Catullus.

Written in red, green and black in an italic hand and gilded by MADELYN WALKER.
Illuminated by JOAN KINGSFORD, 1929. *By courtesy of Mrs St John Hornby.*
(Size 8 in. × 5¼ in.)

H ïc haedos depone, tamen veniemus in urbem.
A ut si, nox pluviam ne colligat ante, veremur,
C antantes licet usque - minus via laedit - eamus;
C antantes ut eamus, ego hoc te fasce levabo.
¶M. Desine plura, puer, et quod nunc instat agamus;
C armina tum melius, cum venerit ipse, canemus.

GALLVS · ECLOGA DECIMA

E X HVNC, ARETHVSA, MIHI CON·
T CEDE LABOREM: PAVCA MEO
R GALLO, SED QVAE LEGAT IPSA
E LYCORIS, CARMINA SVNT DI·
M CENDA: NEGET QVIS CARMINA
V GALLO? SIC TIBI, CVM FLV·
M CTVS SVBTERLABERE SICANOS

D oris amara suam non intermisceat undam,
I ncipe; sollicitos Galli dicamus amores,
D um tenera attondent simae virgulta capellae.
N on canimus surdis, respondent omnia silvae.
Q VAE nemora aut qui vos saltus habuere, puellae
 Naïdes, indigno cum Gallus amore peribat ?
N am neq; Parnasi vobis iuga, nam neq; Pindi
V lla moram fecere, neque Aonie Aganippe.
I llum etiam lauri, etiam flevere myricae,
P inifer illum etiam sola sub rupe iacentem

M aenalus, et gelidi fleverunt saxa Lycaei.
S tant et oves circum - nostri nec paenitet illas,
N ec te paeniteat pecoris, divine poeta:
E t formosus ovis ad flumina pavit Adonis ~
V enit et upilio, tardi venere subulci,
V vidus hiberna venit de glande Menalcas.
O mnes unde amor iste rogant tibi ? Venit Apollo:
G alle, quid insanis ? inquit. Tua cura Lycoris
P erque nives alium perque horrida castra secuta est.
V enit et agresti capitis Silvanus honore,
F lorentis ferulas et grandia lilia quassans.
P an deus Arcadiae venit, quem vidimus ipsi
S anguineis ebuli bacis minioque rubentem:
E cquis erit 'modus ? inquit. Amor non talia curat:
N ec lacrimis crudelis Amor nec gramina rivis
N ec cytiso saturantur apes nec fronde capellae.
T ristis at ille tamen cantabitis, Arcades inquit,
M ontibus haec vestris, soli cantare periti
A rcades. O mihi tum quam molliter ossa quiescant,
V estra meos olim si fistula dicat amores
A tque utinam ex vobis unus vestrique fuissem
A ut custos gregis aut maturae vinitor uvae.
C erte sive mihi Phyllis sive esset Amyntas
S eu quicumque furor ~ quid tum, si fuscus Amyntas ?
E t nigrae violae sunt et vaccinia nigra ~
M ecum inter salices lenta sub vite iaceret;
S erta mihi Phyllis legeret, cantaret Amyntas.

ART

is the expression by man of his pleasure in labor. I do not believe he can be happy in his labor without express ing that happiness; and especially is this so when

Virgil: Eclogues and Georgics.
Writing and gilding by ALFRED FAIRBANK,
illuminating by LOUISE POWELL, *1932 to 1939.*
By courtesy of Mrs St John Hornby.
(Size 12 in. × *8 in.)*

ERNST DETTERER
Quotation from William Morris.
Written in a Foundational hand, 1917.
By courtesy of Mr James Hayes.
(Size 9 in. × *11¼ in.)*

M. C. OLIVER

Extract from The Dignitie of Man *written in black in a sharpened italic hand*

GOD

From "The Dignitie of Man" is the Fountaine of all vertue and duty. By Anthony Nixon 1612

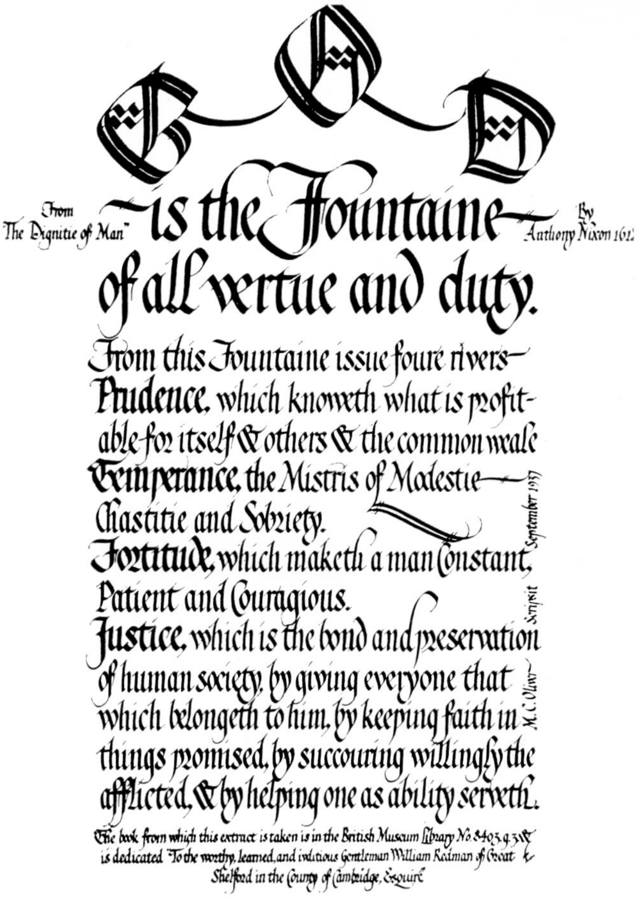

From this Fountaine issue foure rivers—
Prudence, which knoweth what is profitable for itself & others & the common weale
Temperance, the Mistris of Modestie—Chastitie and Sobriety.
Fortitude, which maketh a man constant, Patient and Couragious.
Justice, which is the bond and preservation of human society, by giving everyone that which belongeth to him, by keeping faith in things promised, by succouring willingly the afflicted, & by helping one as ability serveth.

The book from which this extract is taken is in the British Museum Library No. 8403.g.3 & is dedicated "To the worthy, learned, and judicious Gentleman William Redman of Great Shelford in the County of Cambridge, Esquire"

M. C. Oliver Scripsit September 1937

JAN van KRIMPEN

Page from an unfinished manuscript. Writing in black, heading in blue, open initial and beginning of second paragraph in red. By courtesy of Mr S. L. Hartz. (Size 22 in. × 9½ in.)

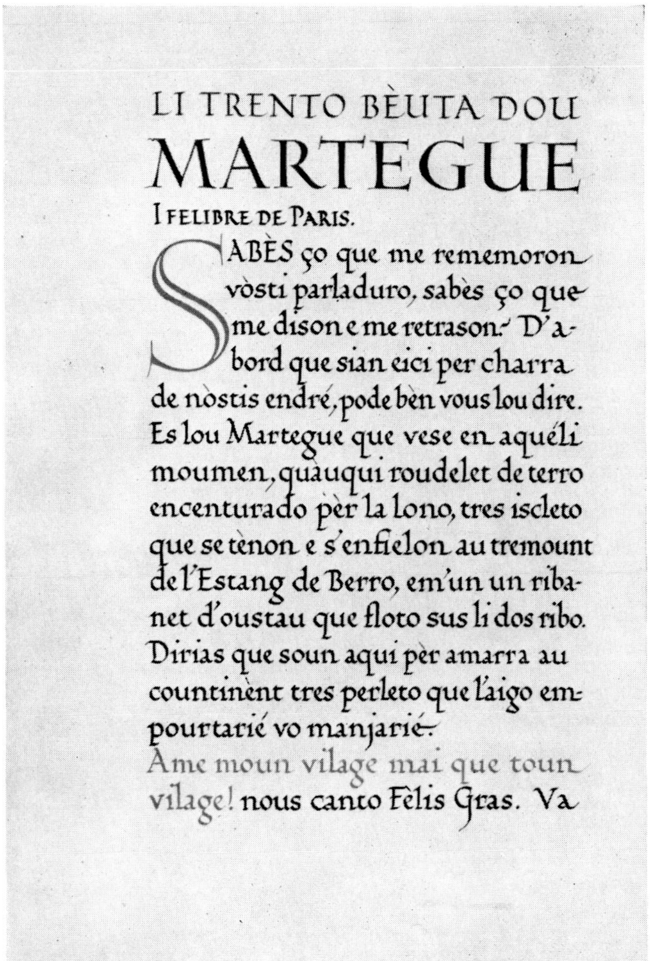

LI TRENTO BÈUTA DOU
MARTEGUE
I FELIBRE DE PARIS.

SABÈS ço que me rememoron vòsti parladuro, sabès ço que me dison e me retrason. D'abord que sian eici per charra de nòstis endré, pode bèn vous lou dire. Es lou Martegue que vese en aquéli moumen, quauqui roudelet de terro encenturado pèr la lono, tres iscleto que se tènon e s'enfielon au tremount de l'Estang de Berro, em'un un ribanet d'oustau que floto sus li dos ribo. Dirias que soun aqui pèr amarra au countinènt tres perleto que l'aigo empourtarié vo manjarié.

Ame moun vilage mai que toun vilage! nous canto Fèlis Gras. Va

PERCY SMITH

Inscription in the possession of Mr Alfred Fairbank

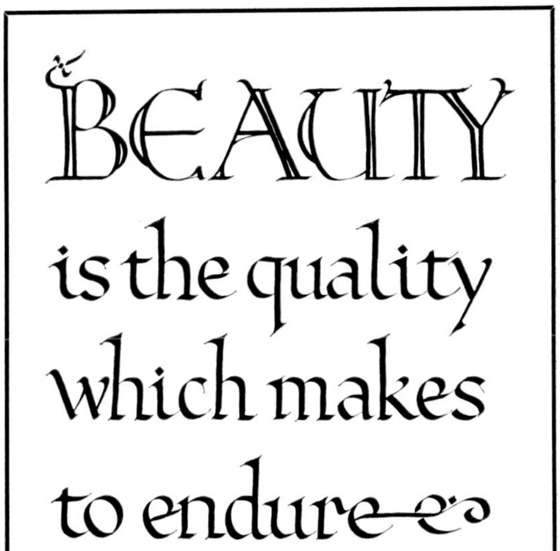

& BEAUTY is the quality which makes to endure

Part of a title-page written and gilded by GRAILY HEWITT,
illuminated by IDA HENSTOCK, *1939. (Reduced)*

DOROTHY HUTTON
Gilded initial of a Patent of Nobility decorated with oak leaves in blue, green and indian red.
Coat of Arms in full colour, the Sovereign's name in vermilion. (Slightly reduced)

A
SA MAJESTE
FREDERIKA
REINE DES HELLENES

LA CONFERENCE INTERNATIONALE DE SERVICE SOCIAL A L'HONNEUR D'OFFRIR LE PRIX RENE SAND 1954,

FONDE EN COMMEMORATION DE SON PREMIER PRESIDENT ET FONDATEUR, EN HONNEUR DE SERVICES EXCEPTIONNELS DANS LE DOMAINE DU TRAVAIL SOCIAL. SA MAJESTE LA REINE, INSPIREE DU DESIR D'ACCOMPLIR LA TACHE DE RECONSTRUCTION SOCIALE APRES-GUERRE, A EU LA PERSPICACITE DE SAISER LES PROBLEMES DE SON PEUPLE ET DE TROUVER LES SOLUTIONS PRATIQUES POUR Y REMEDIER. ELLE A INSPIREE PAR SA FOI ET SON ENERGIE PERSONELLE SES COLLABORATEURS; SON EXEMPLE ET SA PARTICIPATION INDIVIDUELLE ONT SOUTENU L'APPEL A LA CONSCIENCE DE PEUPLE GREC ET DU MONDE ENTIER POUR METTRE LES MOYENS NECESSAIRES A SA DISPOSITION. LES TRAVAUX DU FOND DE LA REINE ONT PERMIS A SA MAJESTE DE RECONSTRUIRE LE TRAVAIL SOCIAL EN GRECE, DE PROMOUVOIR ET AMELIORER SES INSTITUTIONS ET SES METHODES ET DE CREER DES NOUVEAUX ORGANISMES DONT LE BESOIN AVAIT ETE CONSTATE. LA RESURRECTION DU SERVICE SOCIAL GREC, SON DEVELOPPEMENT ET SON AFFILIATION AU TRAVAIL INTERNATIONAL SONT DUES A L'INSPIRATION ET L'EFFORT DE SA MAJESTE LA REINE. EN LUI OFFRANT LE PRIX RENE SAND 1954 LA CONFERENCE INTERNATIONALE DE SERVICE SOCIAL A VOULU NON SEULEMENT ACCENTUER LES MERITES EXCEPTIONNELS DE SA MAJESTE MAIS EN MEME TEMPS EN SA GRACIEUSE PERSONNE HONORER LE PEUPLE GREC, QUI S'EST REMIS SI ADMIRABLEMENT APRES LES CALAMITES DE LA GUERRE ET DES SEISMES.

G. Haynes, President

VIII CONFERENCE INTERNATIONALE DE SERVICE SOCIALE MUNICH AOUT 1956

MARGARET ALEXANDER
Address to Her Majesty Frederika Queen of the Hellenes from the International Social Service, 1956.
Transcribed and illuminated on vellum; framed. (Size 20 in. × 14 in.)

49

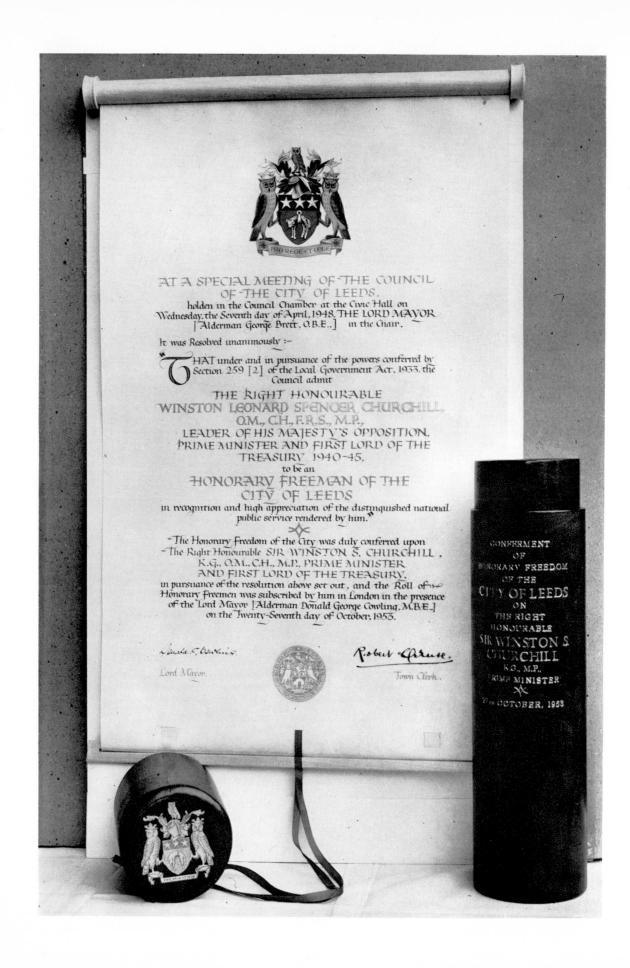

T. W. SWINDLEHURST
*Freedom Scroll presented to
Sir Winston S. Churchill, by the
City of Leeds, 1953. (Reduced)*

DOROTHY MAHONEY
*The Royal Academy's Address presented
on the occasion of the celebrations of the
Royal Society's Tercentenary.
Written in black on vellum, the word
Greetings in vermilion. Ebony roller with
carved ivory ends. Ribbon red.
By courtesy of the Royal Society.
(Size 28 in. × 12½ in.)*

TO THE PRESIDENT AND FELLOWS OF THE ROYAL SOCIETY OF LONDON

GREETINGS

The President and Members of the Royal Academy of Arts in London have great pleasure in congratulating your illustrious Society on the completion of three hundred years of its famous services to the advancement of the natural sciences, and in offering their tribute of cordial good wishes for its continued prosperity and prestige through many centuries yet to come.

The Royal Academy of Arts is mindful of its friendly relations with your Society in Somerset House and Burlington House for most of the past two centuries, and it recalls with pride that four of its Presidents and five other of its Members have been honoured with the Fellowship of the Royal Society; and also that distinguished men of Science, as Professors of Anatomy & Chemistry in the Royal Academy, have regularly given the benefit of their teaching to the Students of its Schools.

On behalf of all the Members of the Royal Academy

PRESIDENT

KEEPER

TREASURER

SECRETARY

SEVERAL OTHER GROUPS of books in the library are worthy of mention. There are, for example, between eighty and ninety 'incunabula' in contemporary bindings. The reference library, which fills a separate room, is particularly noteworthy. Rich, as one would expect in the standard works on manuscripts and bindings, it also embodies two special collections to which Major Abbey has paid particular attention. He has assembled a set of the publications of the Roxburghe Club, which is now nearing completion and which includes a considerable number printed on vellum; and, as befits a collector who has himself produced a noble series of catalogues, he has been energetic in the acquisition of library catalogues, especially those which have been privately-printed in small numbers.

This impressive series of the records of past bibliophily is by no means the least interesting feature of Major Abbey's library, which must in its entirety, rank AS ONE OF THE MOST REMARKABLE IN PRIVATE HANDS TODAY.

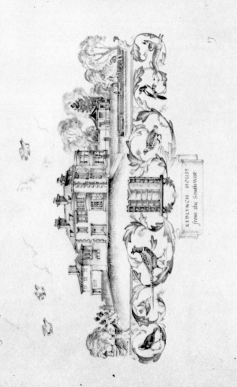

DOROTHY HUTTON · Page from a manuscript book.
The Library of John Roland Abbey.
By courtesy of Major J. R. Abbey. (Reduced)

IDA HENSTOCK · Freedom of the Borough of Bury St Edmunds. Written and illuminated on vellum, 1953. (Reduced)

SACRARIUM REGIS · CUNABULA LEGIS

BOROUGH OF BURY ST EDMUNDS

KNOW ALL MEN BY THESE PRESENTS that at a SPECIAL MEETING of the COUNCIL of the BOROUGH OF BURY SAINT EDMUNDS held in the ABBEY GARDENS, BURY ST EDMUNDS on Saturday, the Nineteenth day of September 1953, it was RESOLVED UNANIMOUSLY That this Council BEING SENSIBLE of the eminent and gallant services and distinguished record of the Corps of the Duke of Yorks Own Loyal Suffolk Hussars, and of the 58th Medium Regiment (Suffolk) R.A.T.A. now amalgamated to form the 358th (SUFFOLK YEOMANRY) MEDIUM REGIMENT R.A. over many years of glorious achievement in the defence of their country since the Napoleonic Wars, and in particular in the cause of freedom in the Wars of 1914–1918 and 1939–1945; and BEING DESIROUS of recognising and fostering the intimate association which has been enjoyed between the Borough and the Corps and Regiment in which so many of its Burgesses have been proud to serve DO HEREBY in pursuance of Section 259 of the Local Government Act, 1933, and in recognition of the aforesaid services confer upon The Suffolk Yeomanry, more particularly known as the 358th (Suffolk Yeomanry) Medium Regiment R.A.T.A. in perpetuity the Honorary Freedom of the Borough of Bury St Edmunds and do hereby admit the Regiment to be an Honorary Freeman of the said Borough accordingly.

Given under the Common Seal of the Mayor Aldermen and Burgesses of the Borough of Bury St Edmunds this nineteenth day of September, 1953

Mayor

Town Clerk

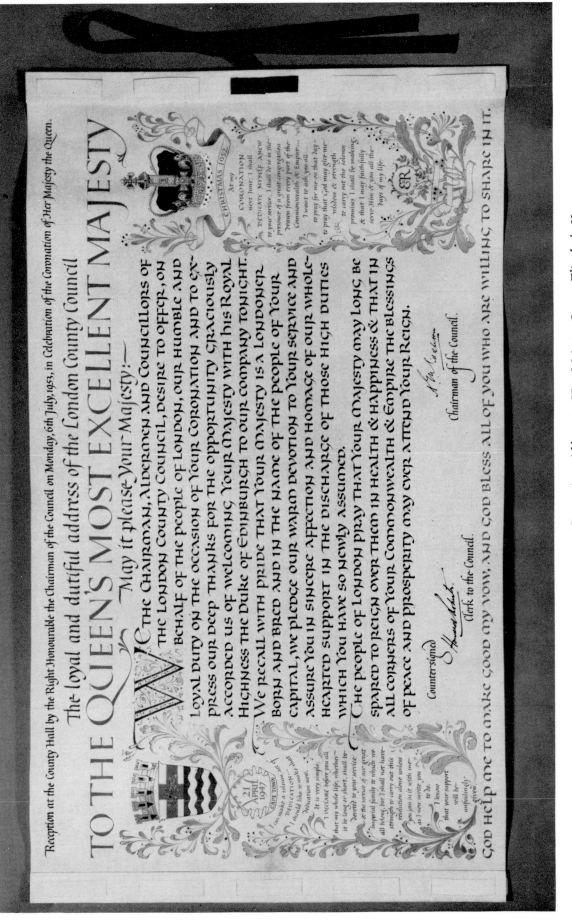

IRENE WELLINGTON · *Coronation Address to Her Majesty Queen Elizabeth II from the London County Council, 1953. Capitals in red between two lines of blue writing, the text in Uncials. The initial W in open blue, decorated in red and gold. The Queen's dedication speeches in brown with matt gold leaves and burnished gold. (Size 28 in. × 17 in.)*

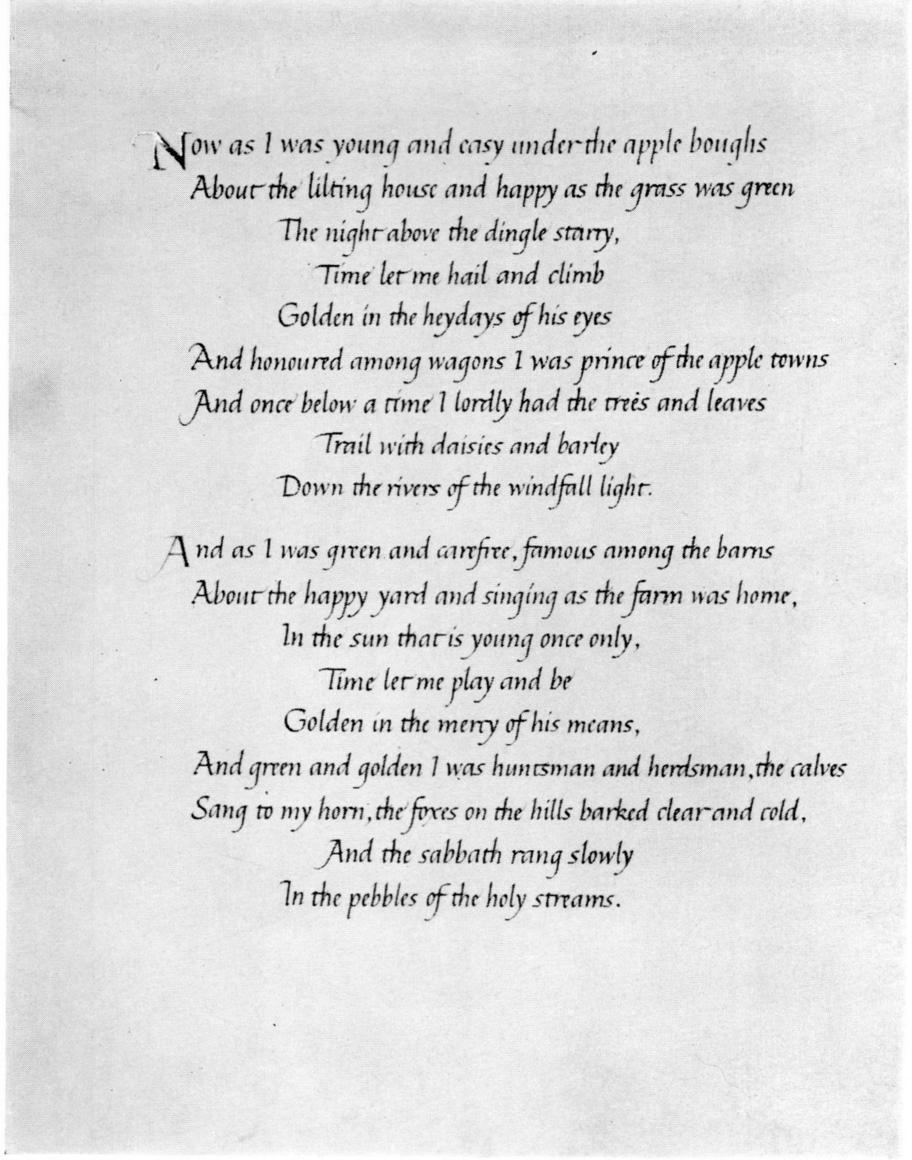

DEUS

OMNIPOTENS
SEMPITERNE
misericordiam Tuam
humiliter imploramus
ut nos coenamque nos-
tram benedicas, et hanc
Universitatem Reginal-
em salvam facias in
Saecula Saeculorum per
IESUM CHRISTUM
DOMINUM NOSTRUM

AMEN

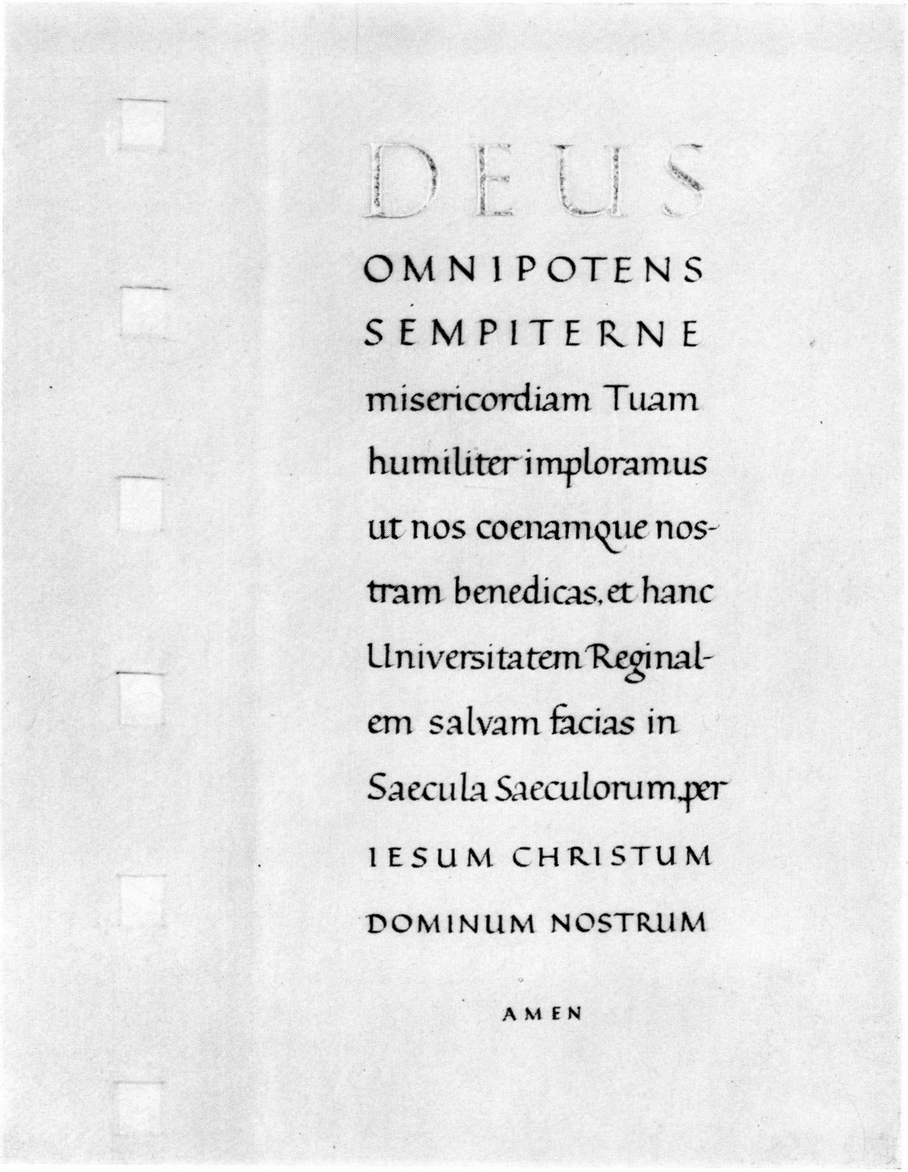

SHEILA WATERS · *Grace of Queen's University of Belfast. A vellum folder. By courtesy of Queen's University, Belfast. (Size 7¼ in. × 3⅝ in.)*

Now as I was young and easy under the apple boughs
About the lilting house and happy as the grass was green
The night above the dingle starry,
Time let me hail and climb
Golden in the heydays of his eyes
And honoured among wagons I was prince of the apple towns
And once below a time I lordly had the trees and leaves
Trail with daisies and barley
Down the rivers of the windfall light.

And as I was green and carefree, famous among the barns
About the happy yard and singing as the farm was home,
In the sun that is young once only,
Time let me play and be
Golden in the mercy of his means,
And green and golden I was huntsman and herdsman, the calves
Sang to my horn, the foxes on the hills barked clear and cold,
And the sabbath rang slowly
In the pebbles of the holy streams.

JOAN PILSBURY · *Page from* Fern Hill *by Dylan Thomas. Written in black on vellum with the initial in burnished gold and the first line in blue. Initial to the second verse in green. By courtesy of Irene Wellington. (Size 8¼ in. × 6 in.)*

M

Ian Cameron MacDonell
Stanislaus McDonnell
Baldwin Childemose MacDougall
John Joseph McDougall
Archibald McDowall
Hugh Stewart McDowell
Alfred Mace
Neil McEachran
Arthur Mark McElhinney
George Edward Henry McElroy M.C. D.F.C.
Victor Henry McElroy D.F.C.
Edward McEvoy
Francis McEvoy
George Clapperton McEwan
Charles William Macey
Alexander McFall
Archibald McFarlan
Foster Murray MacFarland
John McFarland D.S.M.
Donald McIntyre McFarlane
Harold Embleton MacFarlane
James McFarlane
James Lennox MacFarlane
Peter Mac Farlane
William McFarlane
William Smith MacFarlane A.C.
Leonard Lawrence McFaul
Thomas Malcolm McFerran
James McGarry

Peter Liddell McGavin
Eustace Joseph McGee
Wilfred Raworth McGee
David Hegler McGibbon
John McGibbon
Douglas McGill
James Andrew McGill
Alexander George McGillivray
Charles Allister McGillivray
Wilfrid Joseph McGinn
Alexander McGregor
Donald Argyle Douglas Ian MacGregor
Donald Mallock McGregor
Thomas Charles Stuart MacGregor
Joseph Alexander McGuckan
Albert McGuinness
Peter McGuire
Thomas Francis McGuire
John MacHaffie
Alexander William McHardy
Lorne Hunter McHarg
James William McHattie
John Egbert Machin
Roland Frank Charles Machin
Thomas Shanks MacIlroy
Julian M MacIlwaine
Edward Phillips McIndoe
Alexander McBain McIntosh
Edward James McIntosh

John McIntosh
Victor Brown McIntosh
David Percival MacIntyre
James Bennett McIntyre
Lorne Howson McIntyre
Arthur William McJanet
Henry Fergus MacKam
Alfred Edwin McKay
Arthur Gordon MacKay
Charles Henry McKay
Douglas Duncan Anderson MacKay
Duncan Ronald Gordon MacKay D.F.C.
George MacKay
Hamish Strathy MacKay
Harry William Mackintosh MacKay
James Ivan McKay
John Alexander MacKay
John Thomas MacKay
John Wood MacKay
Malcolm William Henry MacKay
Robert McKay
Hugh McKenna
James McKenna
Justin Morell McKenna
Kenneth Mac Kenson
Adrian Somerset MacKenzie
Alec Dudley MacKenzie
Alexander McKenzie

Colin Roy MacKenzie D.S.O.
Donald Albin MacKenzie M.M.
Douglas Fraser Mac Kenzie
Ernest Alexander MacKenzie
Ewen Cameron MacKenzie
George Osborne MacKenzie
Gordon William McKenzie
Helen MacKenzie
Ivan Emilio Mario MacKenzie
John MacKenzie
Keith Ingleby MacKenzie
Seaforth William McKenzie
Thomson MacKenzie
John Alexander Hunter McKeown
Robert Dudley Wilson McKergow
William Archibald Struthers McKerrell
Edward Reeves Mackey
William James Mackey
Andrew Oliver McKie
James McKie
James Matthew Mackie D.F.M.
Rolfe McKiel
John Nelson Burdette McKim
Alexander McKimmie
Duncan McKinnon
Joseph Francis McKinnon
Charles Mackintosh
Lawrence Hill Willson McKisack
Wilfrid Earl McKissock

Royal Air Force Books of Remembrance, St Clement Danes Church.

Pages of Volume I written by SHEILA WATERS to the design and under the direction of Alfred Fairbank, 1961.
By courtesy of the Air Council and the Managing Trustees of St Clement Danes
(R.A.F.) Appeal Fund. (Size 16¾ in. × 12 in.)

ROYAL HORSE GUARDS
ROLL OF OFFICERS

Captain Basil Sheridan, Marquess of Dufferin & Ava
141136 Field Broadcast Unit · Burma · 25 March 1945

Major John Henry George, Earl of Erne
38699 Attached 12th Lancers · France & Belgium · 23 May 1940

Lieut. Michael David Agnew Evans
219282 1st Household Cavalry Regiment · Middle East · 27 December 1942

Lieut. David Hubert Harvey-Williams
315919 2nd Household Cavalry Regiment · North West Europe · 19 April 1945

Lt. Col. Malcolm Archibald Albert Little
27133 44th Reconnaissance Regiment · Italy · 5 October 1944

Captain Edward Christian Frederick Nutting
73081 1st Household Cavalry Regiment · Middle East · 29 January 1943

Lieut. Anthony David Potter
267980 2nd Household Cavalry Regiment · North West Europe · 19 July 1944

Major Richard Algernon Frederick Lord Sudeley
45143 Commando · At Sea · 26 August 1941

Lieut. Robert Francis Sutherland Tudsbery
189793 1st Household Cavalry Regiment · North West Europe · 30 April 1945

ROLL OF OTHER RANKS

Corporal of Horse Frank Lawrence Allenby
305020 2nd Household Cavalry Regiment · Normandy · 2 August 1944

Trooper Edward John George Arris
305650 2nd Household Cavalry Regiment · Normandy · 19 July 1944

Trooper Frank Grenville Ashcroft
305290 1st Household Cavalry Regiment · Palestine · 24 September 1942

Trooper John David Baker
306008 Household Cavalry Training Regiment · United Kingdom · 20 Feb 1945

Lance Corporal of Horse Robert Oxley Barnes
305253 2nd Household Cavalry Regiment · United Kingdom · 15 June 1944

Lance Corporal Kenneth Barnes
305583 2nd Household Cavalry Regiment · Normandy · 18 July 1944

Trooper Bryan Rupert Beckett
7948780 Officer Cadet Training Unit (RAC) Sandhurst · U.K. · 11 March 1943

Corporal of Horse Leslie Arthur Bunce
304956 1st Household Cavalry Regiment · Palestine · 7 June 1941

Trooper Donald Cameron
174165 1st Household Cavalry Regiment · Germany · 30 April 1945

Corporal of Horse Percy Frederick Clark
305249 2nd Household Cavalry Regiment · Germany · 25 April 1945

JOAN PILSBURY · *Roll of Honour of the Household Cavalry. Designed by Irene Wellington, executed by Joan Pilsbury on vellum. Names written in black, the italic lines in red. Burnished gold heading, sub-headings in blue. Badge in full colour and burnished gold. (Size of double opening 18 in. × 12 in.)*

PAT RUSSELL · *Freedom Certificate. Written on vellum in black, red, blue-green and shell gold. Arms in full colour. By courtesy of Philip Noel-Baker, Esq. (Size 17 in. × 6 in.)*

COUNTY BOROUGH OF DERBY

At a Special Meeting of the Council holden at the Assembly Rooms in Derby on Thursday, the 17th day of March One thousand nine hundred and sixty · It was resolved that The Right Honourable

Philip John Noel-Baker, P.C., M.P.

be admitted an *Honorary Freeman* of the Borough

in recognition of the award to him of the Nobel Peace Prize for the year One thousand nine hundred and fifty nine, of eminent services rendered by him to the Borough as one of its representatives in Parliament over a period exceeding twenty three years and to the nation as a Member of Parliament, a Minister of the Crown and its representative on many international occasions and of his lifelong devotion to the cause of world peace and disarmament.

G. A. Collier — Mayor
G. H. Early Jones — Town Clerk

HATHAIR

Rectors of Chillenden

GEORGE THOMSON
Heading from a framed panel of the Lord's Prayer in Gaelic

JOHN WOODCOCK
Heading from a framed panel recording the names of the Rectors of Chillenden

T. W. SWINDLEHURST
Bookplate for Leeds City Arts Club Library

DOROTHY MAHONEY
*Detail from a panel in King's College Chapel,
Cambridge, recording names of Provosts, Fellows
and others buried in the chapel and vaults.
Heading and names in black Uncials,
Coat of Arms in full colour.
By courtesy of the Bursar of King's College*

NOMINA PRAEPOSITORUM COLLEGII REGALIS

WILLIAM MILLINGTON	1441
JOHN CHEDWORTH	1447
ROBERT WODELARKE	1452
WALTER FIELD	1479
JOHN DOGGET	1499
JOHN ARCENTINE	1501
RICHARD HATTON	1508
ROBERT HACUMBLEN	1509

European Carpets

from
BRITAIN
DENMARK
SWEDEN
NORWAY
GERMANY
POLAND
and many other countries

ON THE 4 TH. FLOOR
SEPTEMBER 29. – OCTOBER 25.

PAMELA WRIGHTSON
Poster for exhibition at Heal & Son Ltd.
Written in tan and white on black in gouache
colour with Boxall Poster pens.
By courtesy of Heal & Son Ltd.
(Size 20 in. × 30 in.)

ANN CAMP
Framed panel in the London County Council
Loan Collection.
Written in a compressed Foundational hand
in black and red.
(Size 16¾ in. × 13¼ in.)

STUART BARRIE
Framed panel. Written in vermilion and black on hand-made paper.
The figure drawn in vermilion.
(Size 18 in. × 12 in.)
(Page 59)

Written by Minnie Louise Haskins before the first World War
as an introductory passage to a poem entitled "GOD KNOWS."

I said to the man who stood
at the Gate of the year, "Give
me a light that I may tread
safely into the unknown".
And he replied: "Go out into
the darkness and put your
hand into the Hand of God.
That shall be to you better
than light and safer than a
known way."

Ann Camp · September 1960

DAVID GARRICK spoke this prologue on the stage of the DRURY LANE THEATRE on September 15th 1747. It was written by Samuel Johnson and has become famous in theatre annals.

In this he said

"Hard is his lot, that here by fortune plac'd
Must watch the wild vicissitude of taste
With every meteor of caprice must play
And chance the new blown bubbles of the day.
Ah, let not censure term our fate our choice,
The stage but echoes back the public voice,
The drama's laws, the drama's patrons give
For we that live to please, must please to live.
Then prompt no more the follies you decry,
As tyrants doom their tools of guilt to die;
'Tis yours, this night, to bid the reign commence
Of rescued nature, and reviving sense;
To chase the charm of sound, the pomp of show
For useful mirth and salutary woe
Bid scenic virtue form the rising age
And truth diffuse her radiance from the stage".

Stuart Barrie 1961

IRENE WELLINGTON
Title-page of manuscript Quartet of the Seasons,
in dark reddish brown with burnished shell-gold decoration.
Names of the seasons written in pink.
By courtesy of Mr Philip Hofer, U.S.A. (Size 9 in. × 7 in.)

IRENE WELLINGTON
Birthday greetings, written and painted on vellum

IRENE WELLINGTON · *Double page opening of* Summer *from the* Quartet of the Seasons. *Written in a mid-blue, with decorations by* MARIE ANGEL. *By courtesy of Mr Philip Hofer, U.S.A. (Size 14 in. × 9 in.)*

PAMELA STOKES
Page from a manuscript book.
Six Shakespeare Sonnets written in German

Christening Book. Written on vellum by
DOROTHY MAHONEY
with decorations by MARIE ANGEL.
By courtesy of William Bell Wisdom, Jr, U.S.A.
(Size 11 in. × 7½ in.)

INVITATION CARDS

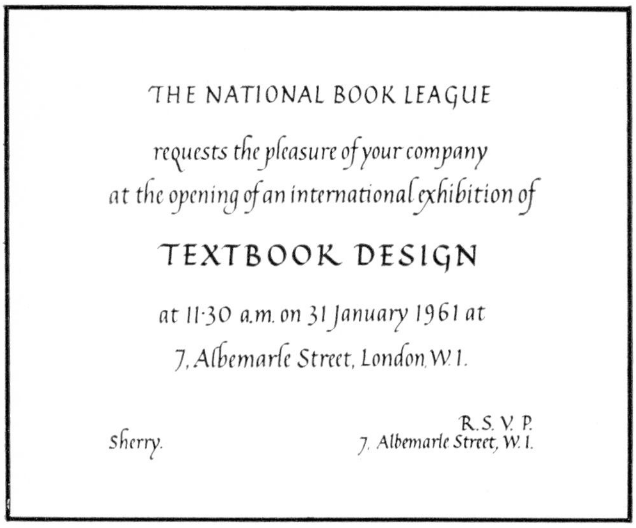

THE NATIONAL BOOK LEAGUE

requests the pleasure of your company
at the opening of an international exhibition of

TEXTBOOK DESIGN

at 11·30 a.m. on 31 January 1961 at
7, Albemarle Street, London W.1.

R.S.V.P.
Sherry.   *7, Albemarle Street, W.1.*

THE SOCIETY OF SCRIBES
& ILLUMINATORS
invite you to the Private View of

AN EXHIBITION OF
Calligraphy
Lettering and
Illuminating
AC

AT THE CRAFTS CENTRE
16·17 Hay Hill · Berkeley Square · W·1
12 OCTOBER 1961
Open until 3rd November

Weekdays 10-5 · Saturdays 10-12·30

1

2

3

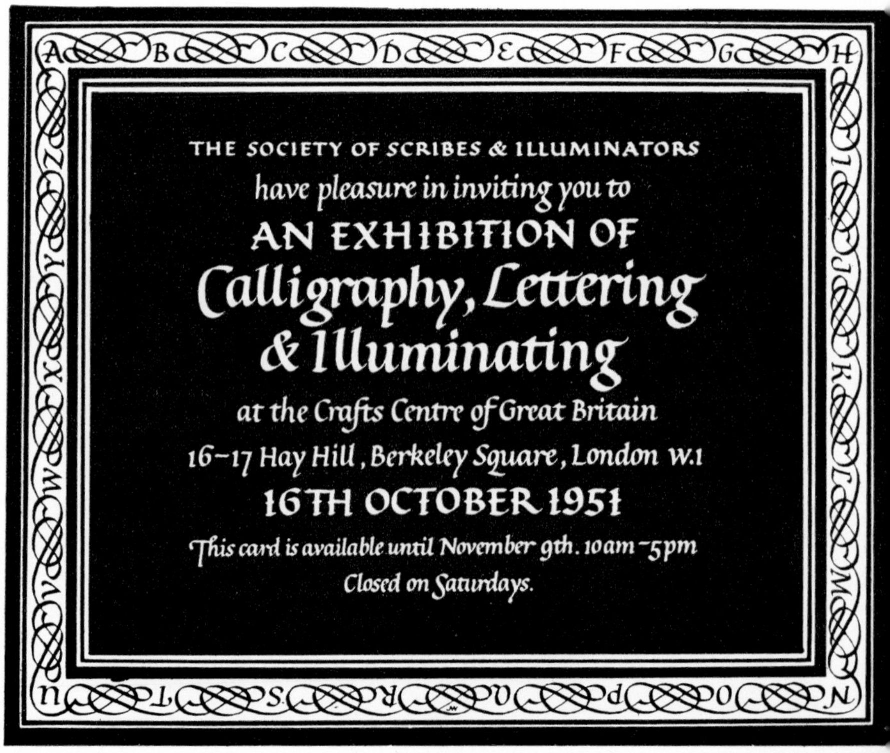

THE SOCIETY OF SCRIBES & ILLUMINATORS
have pleasure in inviting you to
AN EXHIBITION OF
Calligraphy, Lettering
& Illuminating
at the Crafts Centre of Great Britain
16–17 Hay Hill, Berkeley Square, London W.1
16TH OCTOBER 1951
This card is available until November 9th. 10am–5pm
Closed on Saturdays.

1   LEWIS TRETHEWEY

2   ANN CAMP

3   JOHN WOODCOCK

THE CRAFTS CENTRE OF GREAT BRITAIN
16-17 HAY HILL, W.1

SUMMER
EXHIBITION
of Fine Crafts

PRIVATE VIEW
May 29th 1956

WEEKDAYS: 10-5 SATURDAYS: 10-12·30
The Exhibition will remain open until 22nd September

1

1 SHEILA WATERS

2 SHEILA WATERS

3 JOAN PILSBURY

2   3

Sir Stephen and Lady Gibson
request the pleasure of the company of

....

at a Reception on Tuesday 13th November 1956
at the Grosvenor House Ballroom . Park Lane . W. 1.
during which there will be a showing of the films —
'Time and the Rocks'
and 'The World and Ourselves'

R. S. V. P. Iraq Petroleum Company Ltd . 214 Oxford Street, London W 1   Reception 6.15pm Carriages 8pm

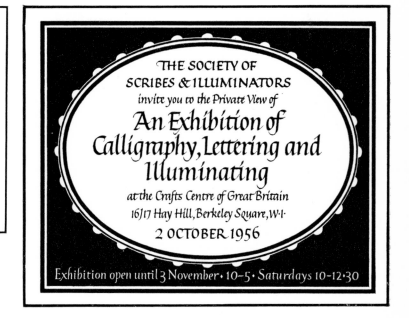

THE SOCIETY OF
SCRIBES & ILLUMINATORS
invite you to the Private View of
An Exhibition of
Calligraphy, Lettering and
Illuminating
at the Crafts Centre of Great Britain
16/17 Hay Hill, Berkeley Square, W·1·
2 OCTOBER 1956

Exhibition open until 3 November · 10–5 · Saturdays 10-12·30

father did not live to see the results that
followed his foresight and generous endow-
ment.

We, the President and Council, desire to place on
record our appreciation of the manner in which
you have administered the Fund. From the
beginning your initiative, untiring energy and
zeal for the cause we all have so much at heart
made success certain and, indeed worthy of
the ideals of the endower of the Fund. Your
personal devotion to the cause has been an
example to us all and we now wish to express
to you our appreciation of your constant
encouragement during recent years — an
inspiration that has helped to enhance that
position of authority and influence which the
Royal Aeronautical Society, after an existence

of some sixty-five years, has now attained.

We wish you happiness and success in that life
of influence and activity which, we are confident,
lies before you.

Patron   *Patron*

President   *President Designate*

Secretary

WENDY WESTOVER · *Address to Harry F. Guggenheim from the Royal Aeronautical Society.*
Gilding by JOAN PILSBURY. *(Size 14 in. × 10 in.)*

HEATHER CHILD · *Double opening from* A Shakespeare Flora.
Written in brown and purple on vellum. By courtesy of Dr J. Shulman. (Reduced)

Violaceae

a. Upper petal.
b. Lateral petal.
c. Lower petal.

d. Upper stamen. x 6

e. spurred stamen. x 6

f. gynoecium. x 6

Viola tricolor
Common Wild Pansy.

Bird's Eyes, Bleeding Heart, Buttery Entry, Call me to you, Cats' Faces, Face & hood,
Fancy, Flamy, Garden Gate, Godfathers and Godmothers, Heartsease, Herb Trinity,
Jack behind the garden gate, Jump up and kiss me, Kitty run the streets, Love-in-
idleness, Love true, Meet-her-i'th'entry-kiss-her-i'th'buttery, Monkey's Face, Pansy,
Pink o'my John, Tickle my Fancy, Two faces under the Sun, Trinity Violet, Wild-
love and idle. From a Dictionary of English Plant Names, Britten and Holland, 1886.

Dicotyledon: # The Violet Family
A Family limited in Europe to the single genus Viola.

VIOLA TRICOLOR
Heartsease, Pansy.

A most variable plant, but easily recognised by the branching
stem, the large leaf-like stipules deeply divided into several
linear or oblong lobes, the central or terminal one the largest,
broadest, and most obtuse, and by the style thickened at the
top into an almost globular oblique stigma. The plant is
glabrous or slightly downy. Leaves stalked, from narrow
oblong to ovate or cordate, always obtuse and slightly crenate.
Flowers purple, whitish, or yellow, or a mixture of these colours;
the two upper pairs of petals slightly overlapping each other,
and usually more coloured, the lower petals always broadest, and generally yellow at the base.
On hilly pastures and banks, in cultivated and waste
places throughout Europe and Asia and abundant in
Britain, especially as a weed of cultivation.
Flowers from spring till autumn.
This is the most variable of all our Violets, and has been
divided into more than a dozen species.

"Yet marked I where the bolt of Cupid fell: It fell upon a little western
flower, Before milk-white, now purple with love's wound,
And maidens call it Love-in-idleness." A Midsummer Night's Dream.

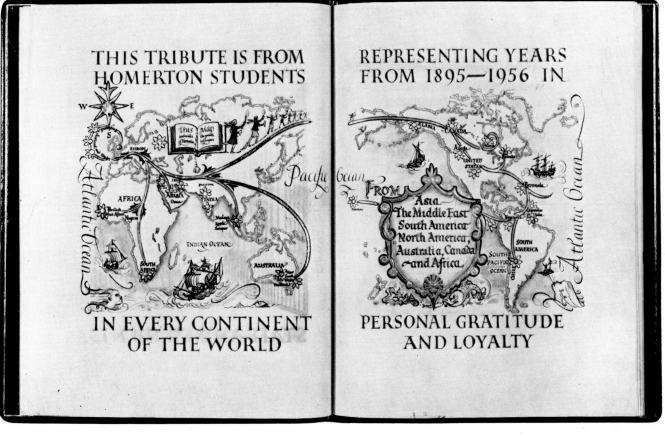

RUTH MARY WOOD
Address to Her Majesty Queen Elizabeth II from the University of Exeter.
Written on vellum in black and red with Versals in blue. (Size 19½ in. × 11½ in.)

GERTRUDE HORSLEY
Tribute to Miss Havergal Skillicorn C.B.E., Principal of Homerton College, Cambridge.
Manuscript written on vellum, 1956. (Reduced)

At a meeting of the Committee of Management of the
ROYAL NATIONAL
LIFE-BOAT INSTITUTION
FOR THE PRESERVATION OF LIFE FROM SHIPWRECK
held at their offices, London, on the 10th December, 1959,
the following minute
was ordered to be recorded on the books of the Institution
That the Gold Medal of the
Royal National Life-boat Institution
be awarded to
Richard Matthew Evans,
Coxswain of the MOELFRE life-boat,
in recognition of his outstanding courage,
determination and initiative, when the
life-boat under his command rescued the
crew of eight of the motor vessel "Hindlea"
of Cardiff, which was in distress about
one and a half miles north of Moelfre
Island, in a north by westerly hurricane
and a very rough sea, on the 27th October,
1959.

President

Chairman   Secretary

RIPON CATHEDRAL

THIS CATHEDRAL CHURCH
WAS CONSECRATED TO THE WORSHIP OF
ALMIGHTY GOD IN THE SEVENTH CENTURY,
AND WAS DEDICATED FIRST
IN THE NAME OF ST. PETER, THE APOSTLE,
AND LATER ALSO IN THE NAME OF
ST. WILFRID, BISHOP OF NORTHUMBRIA
AND FOUNDER OF THIS CHURCH.

REMEMBER YOU ARE STANDING ON HOLY GROUND
because here for well nigh 1300 years our forefathers have
worshipped God, and have confessed their faith in
Jesus Christ, our Crucified, Risen, and Ascended Lord.

AS YOU GO ROUND THIS HALLOWED BUILDING
read in its stones the story of the past, ponder well its lessons
and think not to leave this House of God without lifting
up your heart in thanksgiving for its Founders & Builders
of the past, and in prayer for those who today minister
and worship within its walls: for your homes, your friends
and yourselves, and for all the Family of God.

The Panelling in this Hall is the gift to the University of graduates and other former students on the occasion of the Centenary of Owen's College as a mark of affection and gratitude

GIFTS WERE RECEIVED FROM THE UNITED KINGDOM [including the Isle of Man, Isle of Wight, Northern Ireland, Isles of Scilly & the Shetland Isles] Argentine, Australia, Brazil, Burma, Canada, Ceylon, Channel Isles, Cyprus, Denmark, Egypt, France, Germany, Gold Coast, Greece, Hong Kong, India, Iran, Ireland, Israel, Italy, Jamaica, Kenya, Netherlands, New Zealand, Nigeria, Northern Rhodesia, Norway, Pakistan, Sarawak, South Africa, Southern Rhodesia, Sweden, Switzerland, Tanganyika, Thailand, United States of America

DOROTHY MAHONEY
Vellum panel for the Hopkinson Room, Manchester University. (Size 17 in. × 15 in.)

WILLIAM GARDNER
Presentation Address to Sir Alfred Herbert,
from the Machine Tool Trades Association

IRENE BASE
Quotation from Areopagitica.
From the London County Council. (Reduced)

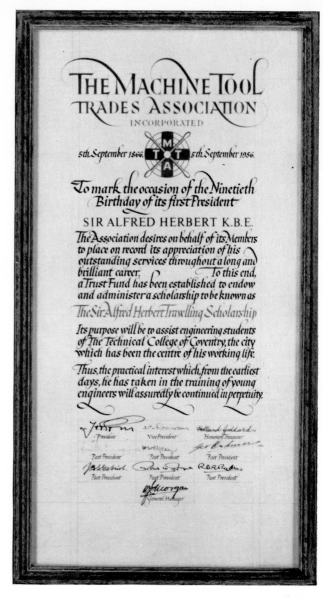

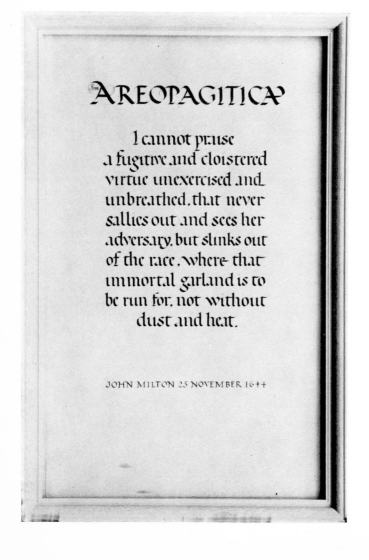

NELZE POZNATI
NITRO ČLOVĚKA,
JEMUŽ NEBYL DÁN ÚKOL.
❡ NELZE POZNATI
ROZUM MOUDRÉHO ČLOVĚKA,
KTERÝ NEBYL Z NIČEHO VYZKOUŠEN.
❡ NELZE POZNATI
SRDCE SPRAVEDLIVÉHO ČLOVĚKA,
NEBYL-LI OCENĚN, KDYŽ SOUDIL.
❡ NELZE POZNATI
SRDCE VĚRNÉHO ČLOVĚKA,
KTERÝ NEBYL O NĚCO POŽÁDÁN.
❡ NELZE POZNATI
SRDCE SOUDRUHA,
NEBYL-LI OCENĚN V DOBĚ HRŮZY.
❡ NELZE POZNATI
SRDCE BRATRA,
KTERÝ NEBYL PROSEN O POMOC
V ÚTISKU.
❡ NELZE POZNATI
SRDCE DÍTĚTE,
DOKUD NEBYLO O NĚCO POŽÁDÁNO.
❡ NELZE POZNATI
SRDCE SLUHY,
JEHOŽ PÁN NEBYL OHROŽEN.
❡ NELZE POZNATI
SRDCE ŽENY,
JAKO NIKDY NELZE POZNATI NEBE +

OLDŘICH MENHART
Proverbs of Ancient Egypt.
Written on vellum in four colours and gold.
(Reduced)

OLDŘICH MENHART
Manifest. Written in two colours.
(Reduced)

PRESIDENT REPUBLIKY
ANTONÍN ZÁPOTOCKÝ
DO PRVNÍHO ROKU
DRUHÉ PĚTILETKY
✳

Dražší spoluobčané, soudružky a soudruzi!

Na prahu nového roku 1956 přeji vám všem, dělníkům, zemědělcům, příslušníkům technické inteligence, pracovníkům vědy, kultury i umění, národních výborů i státní správy, všem veřejným funkcionářům, příslušníkům ozbrojených sil, naší mládeži i dětem mnoho úspěchů při plnění úkolů, které nás čekají v nastávajícím roce.

✳

Letošním rokem začínáme druhou pětiletku. Úkoly, které druhý pětiletý plán staví před naši průmyslovou i zemědělskou výrobu, nejsou malé. Máme však všechny důvody i předpoklady být přesvědčeni, že úkoly roku 1956 splníme s ještě větším zdarem a úspěšněji, než jsme splnili úkoly let minulých.

✳

Věřím, že ubráníme mír, věřím, že splníme naše cíle a plány, věřím ve šťastnou budoucnost naší vlasti a jejího lidu.

✳

Z NOVOROČNÍHO PROJEVU
DNE 1. LEDNA 1956.

CATHARINE FOURNIER
Genuit Puerpera Regem. In black with brown initials and line finishings. (Size 17 in. × 14 in.)

BYRON J. MACDONALD · *Twenty-third Psalm written in black with initial Y in red, 1957*

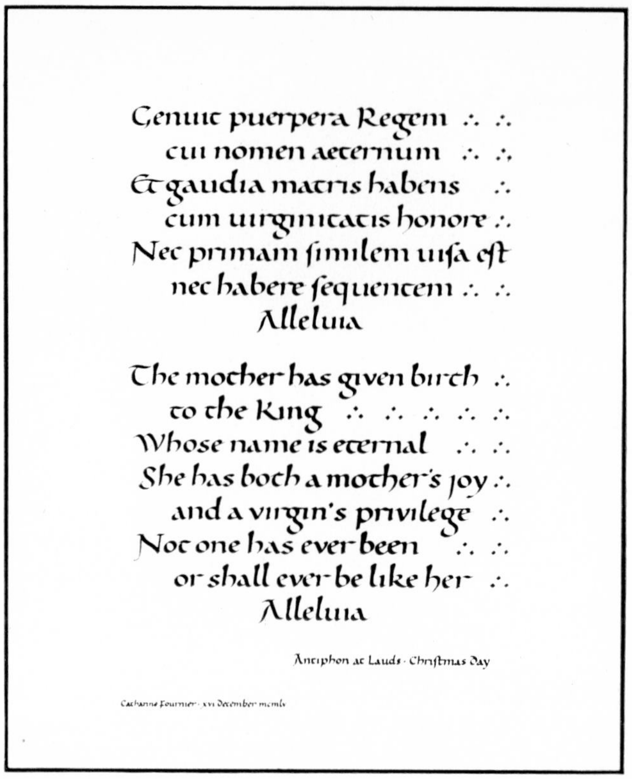

Genuit puerpera Regem ∴ ∴
cui nomen aeternum ∴ ∴
Et gaudia matris habens ∴
cum uirginitatis honore ∴
Nec primam similem uisa est
nec habere sequentem ∴ ∴
Alleluia

The mother has given birth ∴
to the King ∴ ∴ ∴ ∴ ∴
Whose name is eternal ∴ ∴
She has both a mother's joy ∴
and a virgin's privilege ∴
Not one has ever been ∴ ∴
or shall ever be like her ∴
Alleluia

Antiphon at Lauds · Christmas Day

Catharine Fournier · xvi December mcmli

The LORD is my shepherd; I shall not want. He maketh me to lie down in green pastures: he leadeth me beside the still waters. He restoreth my soul: he leadeth me into the paths of righteousness for his name's sake.

Yea, though I walk through the valley of the shadow of death, I will fear no evil: for thou art with me; thy rod and thy staff they comfort me. Thou preparest a table before me in the presence of mine enemies: thou anointest my head with oil: my cup runneth over. Surely goodness and mercy shall follow me all the days of my life: and I will dwell in the house of the LORD for ever.

Heilige Schrift

der HERR
lasse euch reich
und immer
reicher werden
an LIEBE
zu einander

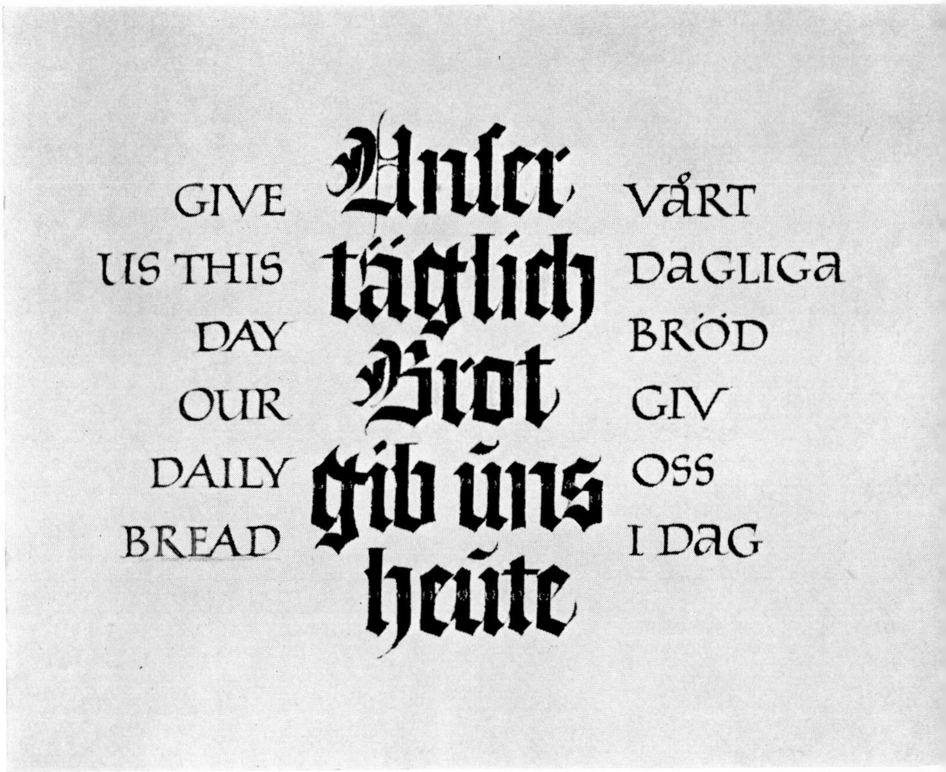

GIVE
US THIS
DAY
OUR
DAILY
BREAD

Unser
täglich
Brot
gib üns
heüte

VÅRT
DAGLIGA
BRÖD
GIV
OSS
I DAG

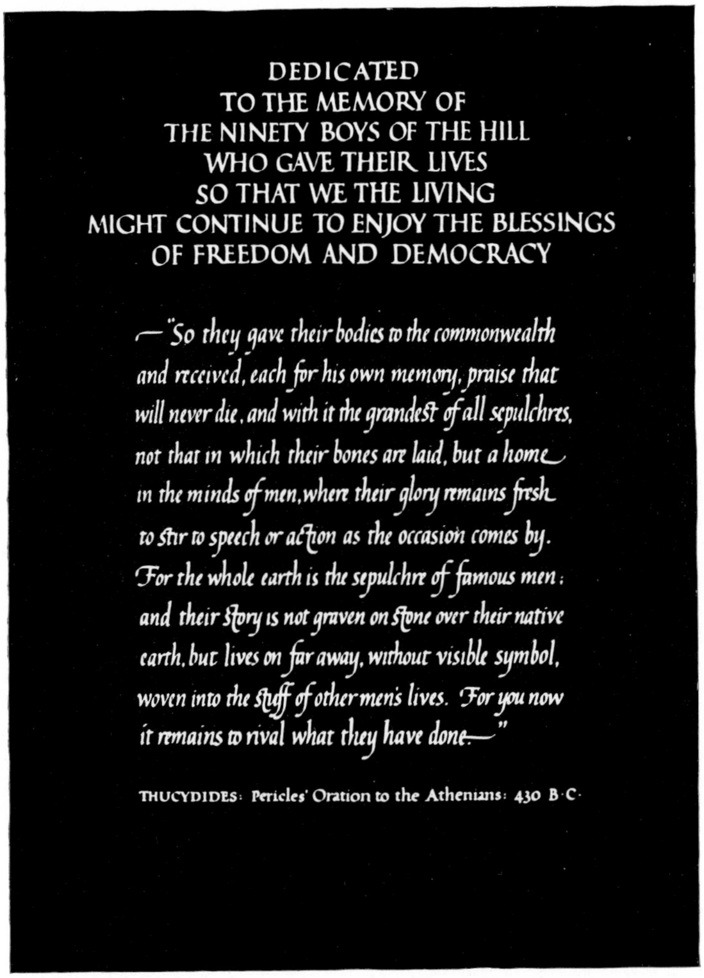

DEDICATED
TO THE MEMORY OF
THE NINETY BOYS OF THE HILL
WHO GAVE THEIR LIVES
SO THAT WE THE LIVING
MIGHT CONTINUE TO ENJOY THE BLESSINGS
OF FREEDOM AND DEMOCRACY

— "So they gave their bodies to the commonwealth
and received, each for his own memory, praise that
will never die, and with it the grandest of all sepulchres,
not that in which their bones are laid, but a home
in the minds of men, where their glory remains fresh
to stir to speech or action as the occasion comes by.
For the whole earth is the sepulchre of famous men:
and their story is not graven on stone over their native
earth, but lives on far away, without visible symbol,
woven into the stuff of other men's lives. For you now
it remains to rival what they have done.—"

THUCYDIDES: Pericles' Oration to the Athenians: 430 B·C·

HANS NIENHEYSEN
Greetings Card in black and ochre

FRITZ EBERHARDT
The Lord's Prayer in English, German and Swedish.
Page from a manuscript book.
By courtesy of the Klingspor Museum, Offenbach

PAUL STANDARD
Dedication page from memorial volume for
Hill School, Pottstown, 1951.
The seven dedicatory lines are in red and black,
the base-line in red, the quotation from
Dr Alfred Zimmern's translation is written in black,
in a set italic. (Size 20½ in. × 15¼ in.)

Då jag en gång jagade på Lesbos, såg jag i Nymfernas lund en syn, den skönaste jag någonsin sett. Det var en målning, en bild ur kärlekens historia. Skön var väl också lunden, trädrik, blomsterfylld, genomfluten av vatten – en enda källa närde allt, både blommorna och träden. Men målningen var ännu behagligare: den gav prov på utomordentlig konst och framställde kärleksöden. Därför kommo också många främlingar, lockade av ryktet, för att tillbedja Nymferna och beskåda tavlan. På denna varsnades födande kvinnor, kvinnor som lindade sina barn, utsatta barn, boskapsdjur som gåvo sådana di, herdar som upptogo dem, unga som ingingo överenskommelser; anlopp av rövare, infall av fiender. När jag sett och beundrat detta och mycket annat dessutom, allt hörande till kärleken greps jag av lust att skriva en text till tavlan. Jag sökte upp en man som kunde förklara bilden, varefter jag utarbetat fyra böcker – en skänk åt Eros...

ERIK LINDEGREN
Example of an italic script. Reproduced by Vara Bokstaver, Göteborg, 1960.

72

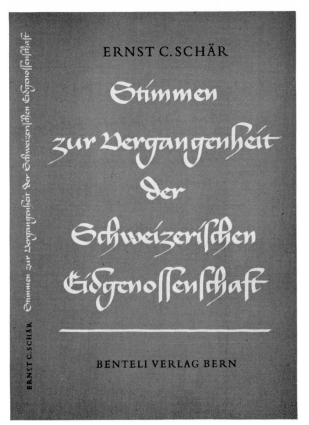

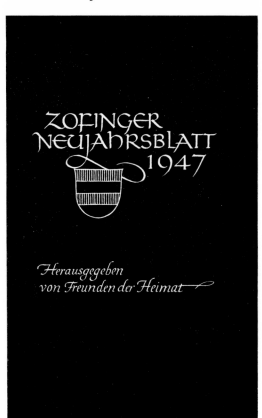

MAX CAFLISCH

EUGEN KUHN

CHRIS BRAND

MAX CAFLISCH

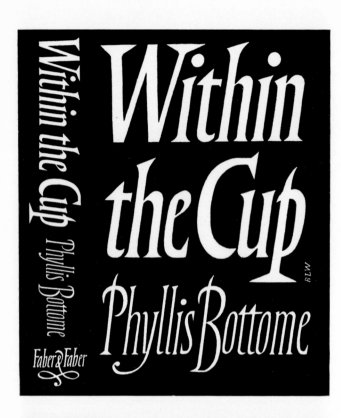

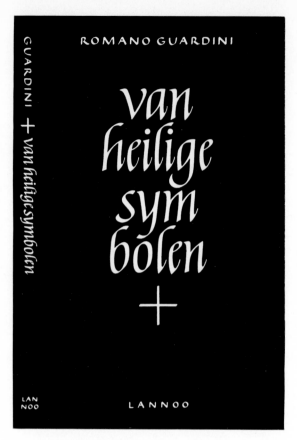

BERTHOLD WOLPE • CHRIS BRAND

GEORGE SALTER • BERTHOLD WOLPE

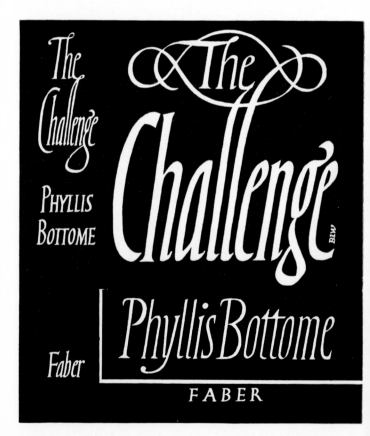

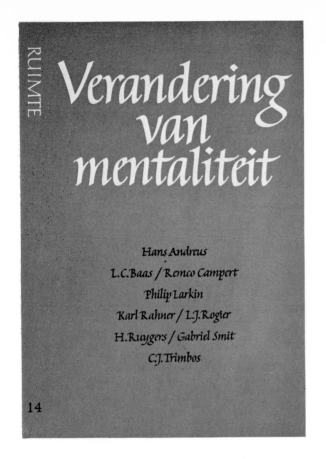

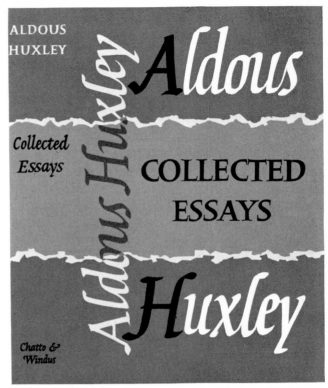

CHRIS BRAND

JAMES HAYES

JOHN WOODCOCK

JOHN WOODCOCK

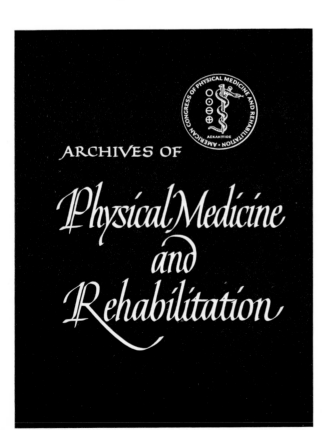

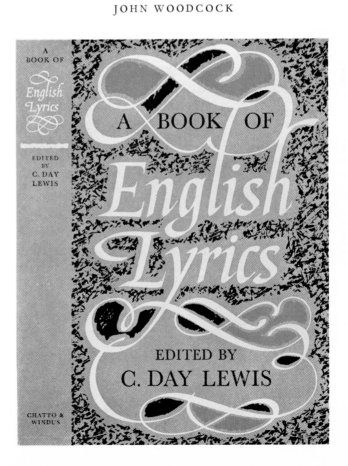

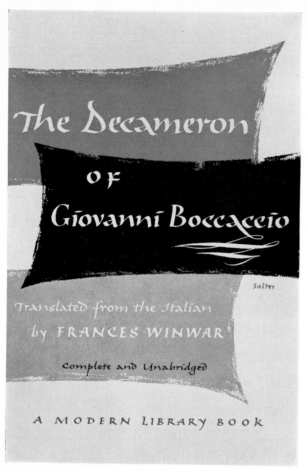

GEORGE SALTER

PAUL STANDARD

PHILIP GRUSHKIN

GEORGE SALTER

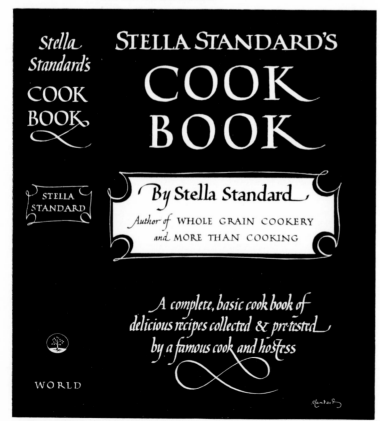

DON EGDON MARGO
Letter heading. Printed in grey on white

DAVID HOWELLS
Compliment slip. Printed white on olive-green.
By courtesy of Newton, Chambers & Co. Ltd.

JAN SCHALKWIJK
Address for the Foundation of Better Handwriting.
Printed in warm brown on green-grey paper.
(Size 8 in. × 6½ in.)

TOM GOURDIE
Detail from a page in
The Puffin Book of Lettering

Some Izal Products
With the compliments of
Newton, Chambers & Co. Ltd.
Thorncliffe, near Sheffield

De stichting ter verbetering van het handschrift,
zich ten doel stellend het handschrift op een hoger
peil te brengen en de leesbaarheid ervan te bevorderen,
verklaart te hebben ingeschreven als :

tegen een jaarlijkse bijdrage van fl.

De stichting geeft hiermede gaarne uiting aan haar grote waardering voor
deze daadwerkelijke bijdrage aan de bevordering van een algemeen belang.

Namens het Bestuur :

Ex Libris
Tom Gourdie

Personal 'ex libris' label
and note-paper
heading

REYNOLDS STONE
Designs made for a set of mugs. By courtesy of Sir Francis Meynell

LLOYD REYNOLDS
Book-plate. Printed in brown on cream

RUDOLPH RUZICKA · *Book-plate*

MANSFIELD PUBLIC LIBRARY
Temple, New Hampshire

Margaret Johnson Bigelow

MEMORIAL FUND

1897–1960

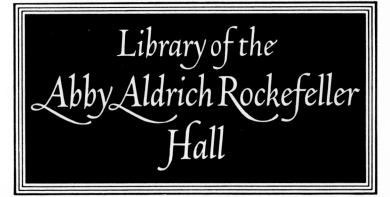

Library of the
Abby Aldrich Rockefeller
Hall

JOHN WOODCOCK · *Title for press advertisement*

GEORGE SALTER · *Title-page for the Composing Room, Inc. 1952*

MAURY NEMOY · *Album cover for Capitol Records*

GEORGE SALTER · *From a title-page for Alfred A. Knopf, 1958*

BYRON J. MACDONALD · *Title for Exhibition Catalogue Cover, 1962*

DAVID SOSHENSKY · *Cosmetic lines. Helena Rubinstein*

RAYMOND F. DA BOLL · *Title for a book designed for the Typophiles, co-ordinating the work of twenty-five American scribes, 1955*

BENT ROHDE · *Name-plate for a printing ink from Danske Fawe-og Lakfabrikker. (Reduced)*

Penguins present National Puffin Week

THIS MONTH we are publishing four new books and
six reprints in our Puffin series for children.
On publication date, 29 October, National Puffin Week will be
launched and booksellers' displays will be supplemented by
special Puffin publicity material
and advertisements in the national press

Four new Puffins

The Story of Jesus
ELEANOR GRAHAM
The life-story of Jesus specially written for
Puffin Books by the Editor of the series 3s 6d

Avalanche!
A RUTGERS VAN DER LOEFF
The exciting story, translated from the Dutch, about a
party of children caught in a series of avalanches 2s 6d

The Lion, the Witch and the Wardrobe
C. S. LEWIS
This magic adventure story, one of the Narnia tales, has
recently been serialized on BBC Children's Hour 3s

The Good Master
KATE SEREDY
The modern continental classic about a town girl
who recovers from measles on her uncle's ranch in the
Hungarian plains 3s

Also these reprints

Bird Watching for Beginners
BRUCE CAMPBELL 2s 6d

The Borrowers
MARY NORTON 2s 6d

A Christmas Manger
JOHN HARWOOD 2s 6d

The Puffin Quiz Book
N AND M. DIXON 2s 6d

The Second Puffin Puzzle Book
W E GLADSTONE 2s 6d

The Puffin Noah's Ark
JOHN MILES 3s 6d

Publication date : 29 October 1959

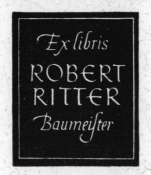

Ex libris
ROBERT
RITTER
Baumeister

EX LIBRIS

OSKAR
HEDINGER

Ex libris
Adam
Schreiber

Ex libris
HANS FINK

Ex libris

Thomas und Annelies
Kuhn-Winkler

EUGEN KUHN · *Book-plates*

OLDŘICH MENHART · *Book-plates*

EX
LIBRIS
VĚRA
VAŇKOVÁ

EX LIBRIS DAGMAR MENHARTOVÁ

EX LIBRIS
JIŘÍ
JAŠKA

JAMES FULLER SPOERRI

Oberlin College
LIBRARY

THE WILLIAM EDWARDS STEVENSON
AND
ELEANOR BUMSTEAD STEVENSON FUND,
established 1957

SIDNEY PAINTER
COLLECTION

The
Johns Hopkins
University

Presented by FRIENDS OF
THE HIGHLAND PARK
PUBLIC LIBRARY ◊ ◊

EX LIBRIS
★
Martha & Stanton
Friedberg

JAMES HAYES · *Book-plates*

*Ex Libris
Palle
Aagaard*

BENT ROHDE · *Book-plate*

REYNOLDS STONE
Engraving by courtesy of Matheson & Co

Jardine Matheson & Co Ltd

VESTIGIA·NULLA·RETRORSUM

The Buckinghamshire Society of Architects
gives this award for excellent craftmanship

Certificate. Lettering by ANN CAMP, designed and engraved by JOHN FARLEIGH

RAYMOND F. DA BOLL
Pattern printed in soft warm grey. Used by the binding department of Newberry Library, Chicago, as end-papers in place of a book-plate

JEANYEE WONG · Book jacket

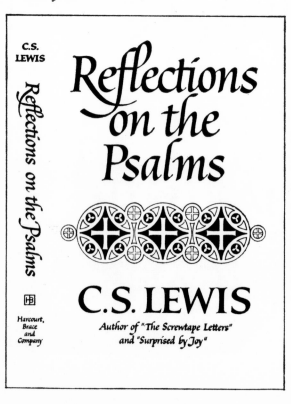

C.S. LEWIS

Reflections on the Psalms

Reflections on the Psalms

C.S. LEWIS

Author of "The Screwtape Letters" and "Surprised by Joy"

Harcourt, Brace and Company

EMMANUEL

From John & Myrtle Skelton & Family 1961 Christmas

Deres assurandør

JOHN SKELTON · *Greetings Card*

BENT ROHDE
Card for the Codan Insurance Company.
Printed in grey on white with capital in black

HEDWIG REINER
A title-page in two colours from
Lettering in Book Art. *(Reduced)*
EUGEN KUHN · *Greetings Card*

BRIEFE
DER
HERZOGIN
ELISABETH
CHARLOTTE
VON
ORLEANS

Glücklich, wessen Leben
einer Wanderung gleicht:
Jubelnder Aufbruch,
kräftiger Marsch,
besinnliche Rast
auf fernschauender Höhe,
zufriedene Heimkehr
des wohlig Ermüdeten
in das weiche Dunkel der Nacht...

CHARLES TSCHOPP

Now having learned the
Alphabet, in order to get a unity in the
script I must advise you that all the ascenders

should be equal as are b d h k l
with their curved & thickened
tops made in the same way as the
beginning of a c l L

Similarly the descenders should be of
an equal length below
the line

& the bodies of all the letters should
be level both at the bottom & the top in
this way as shewn
here

Aabcdefmfmgmbiklmnopqrsstuftumvxyz

A page from Arrighi's La Operina, translated and transcribed by ANNA HORNBY, 1956

A page from The First Writing Book, La Operina, by Ludovico degli Arrighi of Vicenza, produced in Rome, 1522

86

Having now come to the letters x y z,
we find that of these the x and y
begin almost in the'
same way,
thus ⌣, crossing in the middle of
the first stroke to make the x, which
in from ought to be no higher than
an a
Let a y be made the same as to height,
in this way
xayayayayayay
of
the z teach yourself to make
it with these strokes as here shown

Sei de følgende linier hvilke bogstaver, der
kan sammenskrives med alle de bogstaver
som følger efter
aa ab ac ad ae af ag ah ai ak al am an
ao ap aq ar as at au ax ay az
Ligesaa kan du gøre med d i k l m n u.
Ligaturerne af c f s ſ t cr
de neden=
nævnte

ct , fa ſſ fi fm fn fo fp fr fu fy,
ſt ſſt
ſſ ſſß ſt, ta tt ti tm tn to tq tr tt tu
ty ty
Alfabetets øvrige bogstaver, nemlig
b g h o g r x y z maa aldrig
sammenskrives med noget efter=
følgende bogstav

A page from Arrighi's La Operina, translated and
transcribed by JOHN HOWARD BENSON, 1955. By
courtesy of Yale University Press

A page of Arrighi's La Operina, translated and transcribed
in Danish by BENT ROHDE. (Den grafiske Hojskoles
Skrifter VII published in Copenhagen, 1959.)

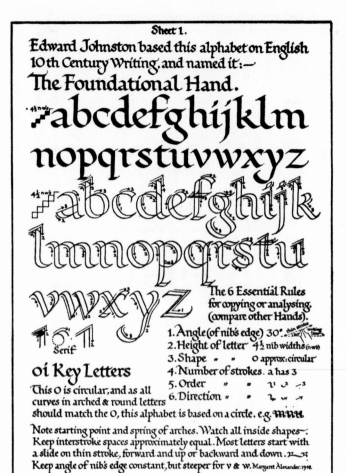

Sheet 1.

Edward Johnston based this alphabet on English 10th Century Writing, and named it:—

The Foundational Hand.

abcdefghijklm
nopqrstuvwxyz

abcdefghijk
lmnopqrstu
vwxyz
16.7
Serif

oi Key Letters

This O is circular, and as all curves in arched & round letters should match the O, this alphabet is based on a circle. e.g. mnu

Note starting point and spring of arches. Watch all inside shapes. Keep interstroke spaces approximately equal. Most letters start with a slide on thin stroke, forward and up or backward and down. Keep angle of nib's edge constant, but steeper for v & w. Margaret Alexander. 1916.

The 6 Essential Rules for copying or analysing. (compare other Hands).
1. Angle (of nib's edge) 30°.
2. Height of letter 4½ nib widths (n-ws)
3. Shape   " " O approx circular
4. Number of strokes. a has 3
5. Order
6. Direction

SHEET 2

CAPITALS FOR USE WITH THE "FOUNDATIONAL HAND," SHOWN ON SHEET ONE IN THIS SERIES

ABCDEFGHIJKL
MNOPQRSTUV
WXYZ AAMMNNWBDHP
EGHMXTWUFIG

ABCDEFGHIJK
LMNOPQRSTUV
WXYZ MUUTUH

WIDE { CGDOQ circular / MW over a square / AHUNVTXZ approx sq. }   NARROW { BEFSY approx ½ sq / IJ under / KPRL slightly over }

ESSENTIAL FORMS (i.e. Skeleton Shapes) should be drawn and studied first:— ABCDEFGHIJKLMNOPQRSTUVWXY Z

LINES OF CAPITALS MAY BE A WHOLE OR ½ LETTER-HEIGHT APART. WHEN USED AMONG SMALL LETTERS THEY SHOULD BE ABOUT ⅔ AGAIN THE HEIGHT OF THE a; SAME HEIGHT AS ASCENDERS (of bdf hkl). To ensure even "Texture" watch spacing of strokes, letters, words, lines on page.

Keep 2 straight strokes far apart ||
  " a straight stroke & curve near IC
  " two curves nearer still X

Margaret Alexander. 1949.

MARGARET ALEXANDER
Two Writing Sheets, based on Edward Johnston's Foundational Hand, 1949.
(Size 13 in. × 9½ in.)

RUDOLPH KOCH · *An alphabet from an A.B.C. booklet*

abcdefghijklmno
pqrstuvwxyz 2
s ß tz ch & 1384

Alternative less formal serifs: ahnpr/npr

ABCDEFGHIJKLMN
OPQRSTUVWXYZZ
Aabcdefghijklmnopqrst
uvwxyz & ?!:; 0123456789
æœ fi ff ffi ffl ry ra ty tw tt ft z

AMNRUW

JOHN WOODCOCK · *Writing Sheet. Roman Capitals and lower-case, one of a set. (Size 14 in. × 9¾ in.)*

WILLIAM GARDNER · *Writing Sheet, Versal Capitals, printed in red. One of a series. (Size 13 in. × 8 in.)*

EXAMPLE № 2 — VERSAL CAPITALS *for use as Initials and as Headings to Scripts*
Pen drawn, usually in colour, and following closely the proportions of the Roman Monumental Alphabet

ABCDEFGHIJKLMN
OPQRSTUVWXYZ &

I Stems waisted

Outer curves sharper than inner curves

OE

Pen held normally for most main stems and curves, but turned for horizontal stems of letters A E F H LT and Z

Some permissable variations and flourishes

 ÆEGJLNR

Decorative medieval styles, overpopularised in the nineteenth century, now not generally used

William Gardner 1961

89

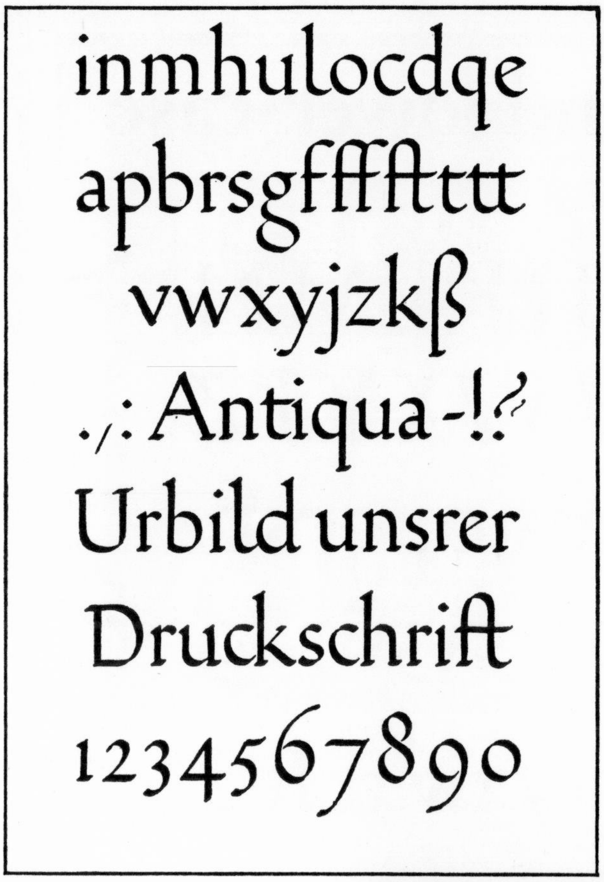

inmhulocdqe
apbrsgfffftttt
vwxyjzkß
.,: Antiqua -!?
Urbild unsrer
Druckschrift
1234567890

JAN TSCHICHOLD
Example from
Schriftkunde, Schreibubungen und Skizzieren

ADRIAN FRUTIGER
An example from Schrift Ecriture Lettering,
showing the development of European letter forms
from the Greek Lapidary Style to Humanistic Cursive,
engraved in wood and reproduced in the form of a folder

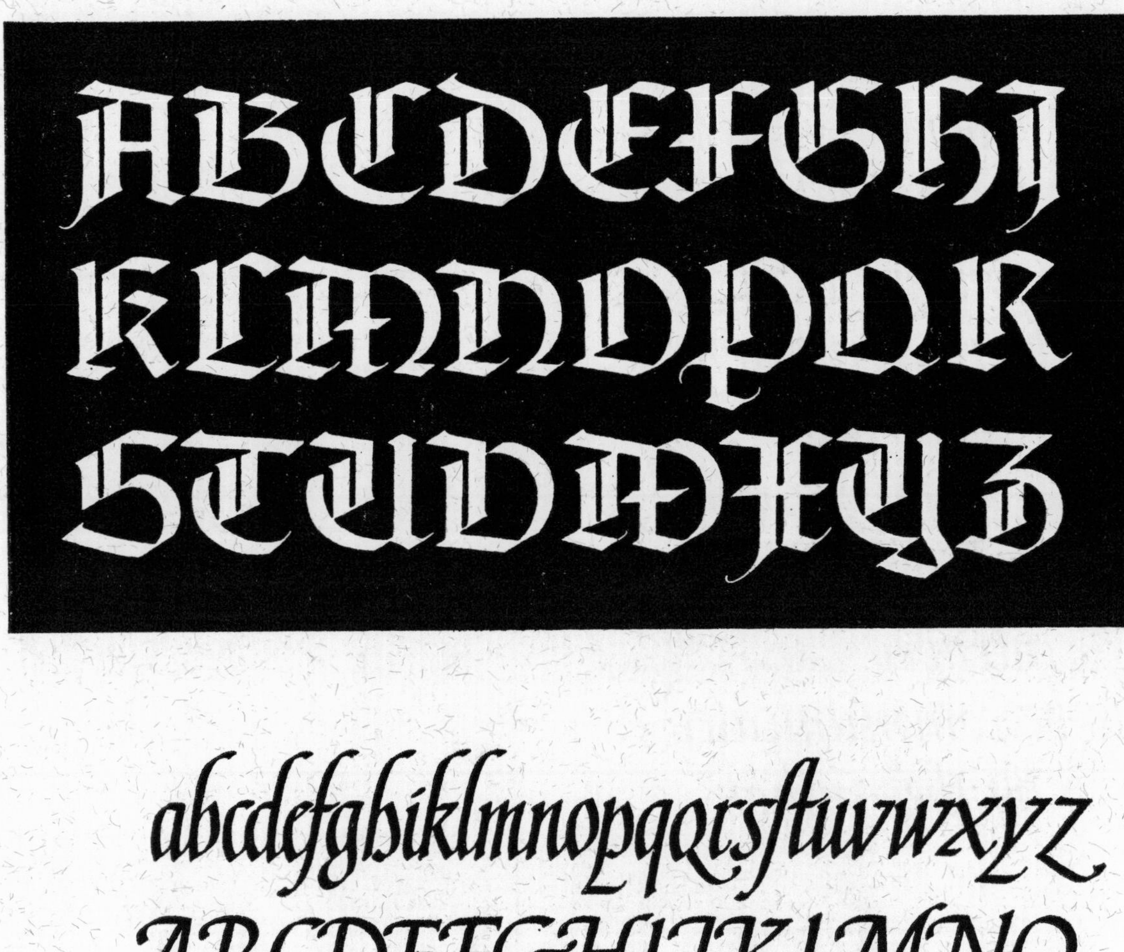

ABCDEFGHI
KLMNOPQR
STUVWXYZ

abcdefghiklmnopqrsstuvwxyz
ABCDEFGHIJKLMNO
PQRSTUVWXY&ZZ

Sedulo curavi humanas actiones
non ridere non lugere, neque de-
testari, sed intellegere

278

WALTER KAECH · *Examples of scripts*

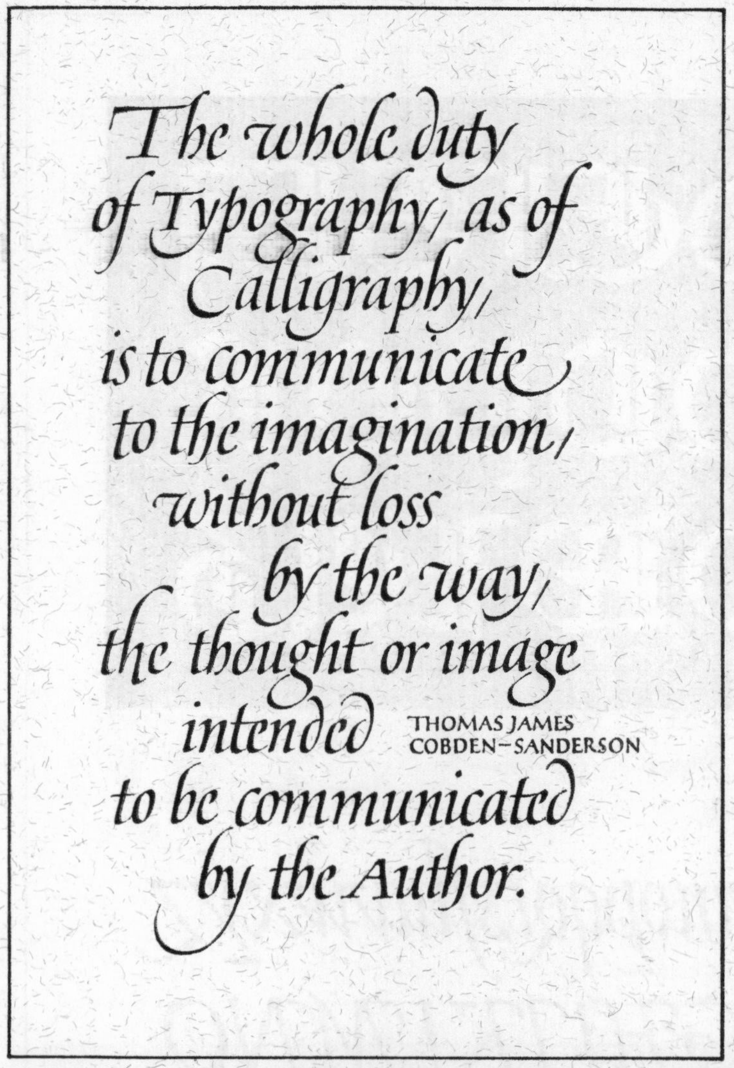

The whole duty
of Typography, as of
Calligraphy,
is to communicate
to the imagination,
without loss
by the way,
the thought or image
intended
to be communicated
by the Author.
THOMAS JAMES
COBDEN-SANDERSON

HERMANN ZAPF
Page of a projected Writing Book with quotations in different languages

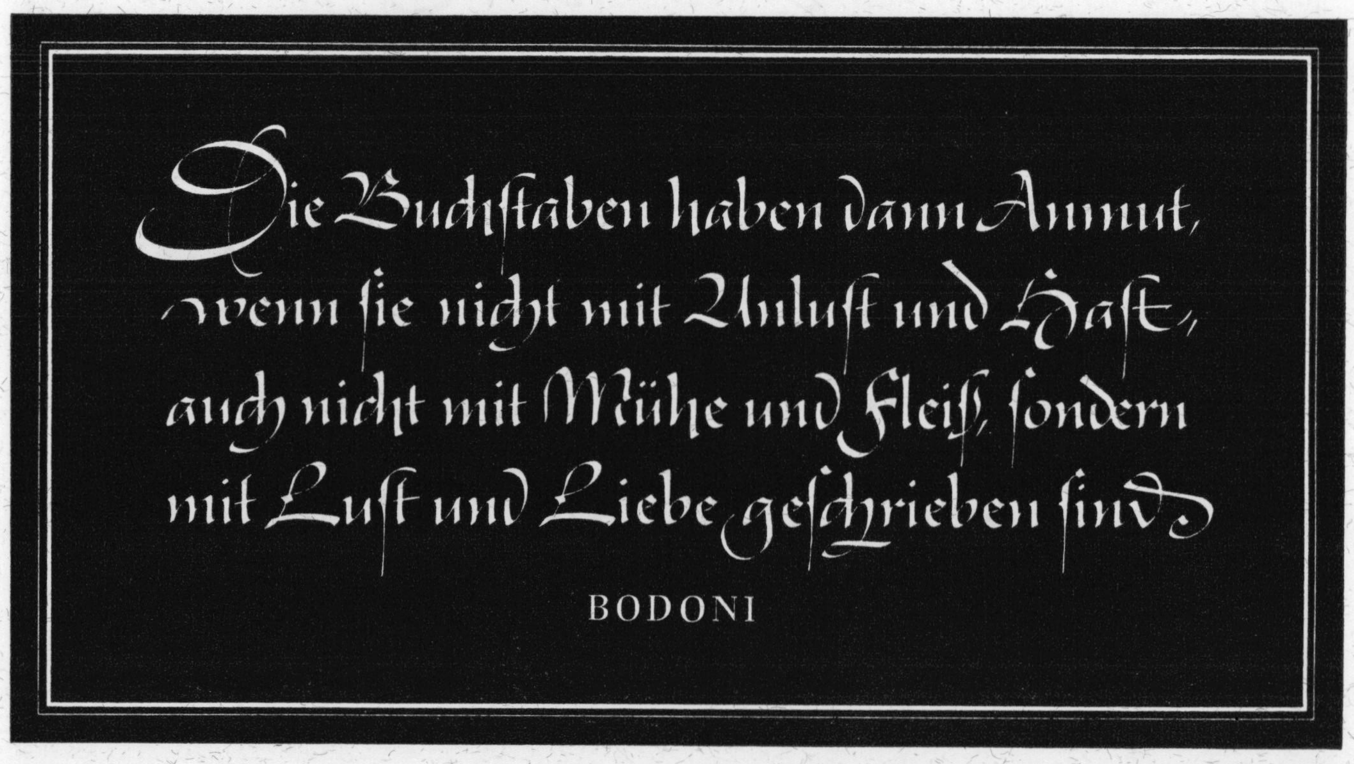

Die Buchſtaben haben dann Anmut,
wenn ſie nicht mit Unluſt und Haſt,
auch nicht mit Mühe und Fleiß, ſondern
mit Luſt und Liebe geſchrieben ſind.
BODONI

HERMANN ZAPF
Page from Pen and Graver, *25 Alphabets and pages of Calligraphy. Cut in metal by August Rosenberger*

AA BB CC DD EE FF GG HH II JJ KK LL MM NN OO PP QQ RR SS TT
UU VV WW XX YY ZZ HAHBHCHDHEHFHGHHHIHJHK
HLHMHNHOHPHQHRHSHTHUHVHWHXHYHZH O
AOBOCODOEOFOGOHOIOJOKOLOMOPOQOROSOTO

UOVOWOXOYOZO PACK MY BOX WITH FIVE DOZEN
LIQUOR JUGS Aam Bbm Ccm Ddm Eem Ffm Ggm Hhm Iim Jjm
Kkm Llm Mmm Nnm Oom Ppm Qqm Rrm Ssm Ttm Uum Vvm Wv&c
Xxm Yym Zzm ..,:;-()!?¨""1234567890 1234567890

ARNOLD BANK
Plate from Lettering Portfolio.
Roman Capitals and Exercises.
Portland, Oregon, 1951.
(Size 11 in. × 8¼ in.)

CHRIS BRAND
Page from Ritmisch Schrijven.
(Size 6¼ in. × 6 in.)

IJ L E F IJ Y L E F
India Jacht Ydel
Lafenis Edel Fruit
Jedereen wantrouwen is dwaasheid,
niemand wantrouwen onnozel,
zichzelf wantrouwen de eerste
stap naar de wijsheid.

13

ABCDEFGHIJKLOMN PQRSTUVWXYZ&BF abcdefghijklmnopqrs tuvwxyzaefigffgkqrti

SEMIFORMAL majuscules and minuscules. The slant from the vertical is 6 degrees and the cant [angle between reed-edge & horizontal writing line] is about 25 degrees. The restrained slant and the compressed counters are the two chief characteristics of semiformal writing. This can be used as a basic model for everyday informal writing.

Roman writing chart no. 3. Catfish Press, St. Ambrose College Davenport Iowa.

1940

FATHER E. M. CATICH
Semi-formal majuscules and minuscules
Roman Writing Chart No. 3. Catfish Press, 1940

ANN CAMP · *The construction of Pen-written*
Roman Letters. By courtesy of Dryad Handicrafts.
(Size 8½ in. × 5½ in.)

MAURY NEMOY · *Majuscules and minuscules*

ABCDEFGHIJ KLMNOPQR STUVWXYZ& abcdefghijklmn opqrstuvwxyz &

abcdef
ghijklm
nopqrst
uvwxyz

Pen angle steeper for diagonal strokes ⌐ approx 45°

&123456
7890.,:;?!

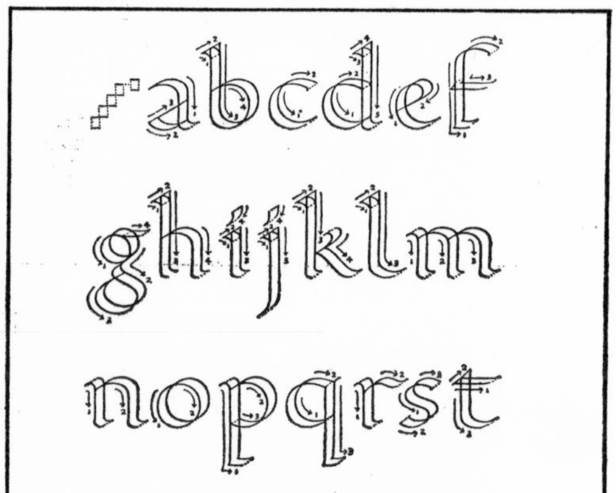

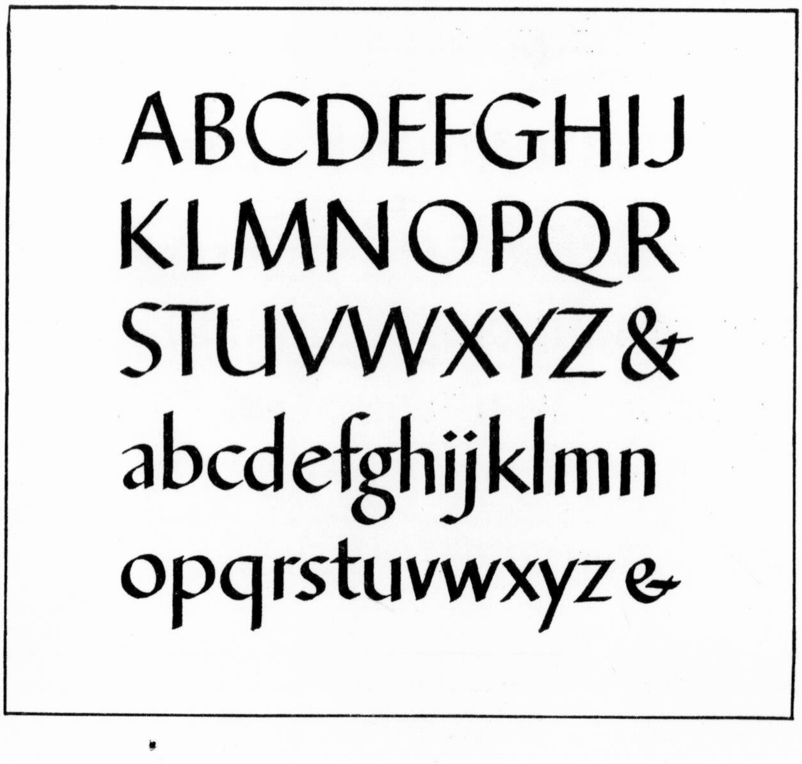

No. 13. a-b counters

ō d́ d́ adgq ʸǫ ợ Ɖ bp

prod able quip dog pig bridge
page squab quad agile brusque
pique barque gape pad adage
drop bag barge depend pod
goad badge borogoves gimble
outgrabe bandersnatch drape
brillig vorpal body Podsnap
13

LLOYD J. REYNOLDS
*Page from Italic Lettering and Handwriting Exercise Book.
Champoeg Press, U.S.A., 1957. (Size 8½ in. × 5¾ in.)*

ALFRED FAIRBANK · *Page from Beacon Writing
Book Six. Published by Ginn & Co., London, 1959.
(Size 8¾ in. × 6 in.)*

CHRIS BRAND
Part of a page from Ritmisch Schrijven

1234
567
890
!?,;:""
& et

MUSIC
Orpheus with his lute made trees,
And the mountain tops that freeze,
    Bow themselves when he did sing:
To his music plants and flowers
Ever sprung; as sun and showers
    There had made a lasting spring.

Every thing that heard him play,
Even the billows of the sea,
    Hung their heads and then lay by.
In sweet music is such art,
Killing care and grief of heart
    Fall asleep, or hearing, die.
        John Fletcher

Index of Calligraphers
whose work is shown in the Illustrations